MARRIAGE
PLANS FOR TWO

Before and After the Wedding

LISA & LENARD TILLERY

Marriage Plans for Two

By Lenard and Lisa Tillery

Copyright ©2022 Lenard & Lisa Tillery

All rights reserved. This book is protected under the copyright laws of the United States of America. This book may not be copied or reprinted for commercial gain or profit.

Unless otherwise indicated, Scripture quotations marked (KJV) and (AMP) are taken from the comparative study Bible: a parallel bible presenting the New International Version, New American Standard Bible, Amplified Bible, King James Version. (1984). Zondervan.

ISBN 979-8-218-01670-8

Royal Kingdom Publishing
www.keyottacollins.com

Presented To

_____

By

_____

Date

_____

Where do we go from here?

- Know your Current Position

- Get Directions

- Develop a Plan

- Follow the Instructions

- Reach your Destination

TABLE OF CONTENTS

PREFACE 1

Chapter 1: "MARRIAGE PLANS FOR TWO" (MP42) 3

Chapter 2: THE SEVEN STAGES 9

Chapter 3: FOUNDATIONS - THE PROLOGUE 31

Chapter 4: FOUNDATIONS - COMMUNICATION 35

Chapter 5: FOUNDATIONS - WISDOM 43

Chapter 6: FOUNDATIONS - LOVE 59

Chapter 7: FOUNDATIONS - COMMITMENT 65

Chapter 8: FOUNDATIONS - SACRIFICE 69

Chapter 9: FOUNDATIONS - TRUST 71

Chapter 10: FOUNDATIONS - HONOR 73

Chapter 11: FOUNDATIONS - INTIMACY 75

Chapter 12: BEFORE YOU SAY "I DO" 79

Chapter 13: WEDDING VERSUS MARRIAGE 83

Chapter 14: WORKING TOGETHER 89

Chapter 15: THE EQUATION 95

Chapter 16: SIMILAR BUT DIFFERENT 105

Chapter 17: OPPOSITES ATTRACT 113

Chapter 18: LIVE RESPONSIBLE 119

Chapter 19: UNCHAINED LOVE 127

Chapter 20: IDENTIFY WHERE YOU ARE 131

Chapter 21: UNTIL THE END 137

Chapter 22: THE MASCULINE MARKER 145

Chapter 23: THE FEMININE FINGERPRINT 151

Chapter 24: Imminent Visualizations 157

BIOGRAPHIES 171

MARRIAGE
PLANS FOR TWO

Before and After the Wedding

LISA & LENARD TILLERY

MP42
MP42
MP42
MP42
MP42
MP42
MP42
MP42
MP42
MP42
MP4
MP42

PREFACE

We dedicate this book to the memory of our pastor, the late Richard V. Allmon, Sr. His instructions and the life we witnessed him live for over twenty-six years while under his leadership led us to write "MARRIAGE PLANS FOR TWO. He was not only a great husband and father, but he was also a profound teacher who loved sharing the glorious gospel of God in word, in deed, and in truth. Jesus blessed him with a myriad of gifts and a personable character. Countless individuals benefited from the infinite knowledge he shared and were impacted throughout his life and ministry. His heavenly and earthly wisdom was responsible for winning many souls to Christ and assisting countless others in achieving a propitious and overcoming Christian life.

He emphasized the importance of having a lifelong common denominator in marriage. A factor that a couple would share interest in throughout their lives. An entity that would not fade over time and would not change as individuals age or alter their life goals. God was his solution, and we advise the same. Adding Jesus and the Word of God to the marriage equation makes problems

PREFACE

easier to manage or solve. It has been said, "A family that prays together, stays together." We are forever thankful for his contributions to our souls and marriage.

With the proper biblical worldview, will power, and work ethic, you can achieve the needed spiritual transformation that leads to spiritual formation and marital realization.

We hope that this marriage manual will inspire you to find practical insights and applications before you marry, and/or during your marriage, which will assist you in your quest for maturity, unity, happiness, and success.

To God be the Glory.

CHAPTER 1

"MARRIAGE PLANS FOR TWO" (MP42)

This "MARRIAGE PLANS FOR TWO" handbook is designed to facilitate long term success in marriage. Careful planning helps couples to get their A.I.M. (Agendas, Intentions and Motives) right before the ceremony, during the wedding ceremony, and throughout the marriage journey.

The wedding ceremony is a time to celebrate the act of marriage. It is an event specifically designed for the happiness of the people (friends and family) who are associated with you and your spouse to be.

The marriage is intimately, holistically, and uniquely designed for the two of you. When planning your marriage, plan and prepare for success. You and your spouse will only have one life to love and make the most of your time together. Always remember that time, not money, is the most precious resource in your lives.

The mystery of marriage is the unification of two individuals becoming one cohesive unit that is loyal to one another. Once the mystery is truly understood it is easier for the couple to work toward the type of relationship that God designed for marriage. Anything inexplicable is hard to comprehend. Clarity is achieved as you learn more about one another. Only by demonstration can you prove that you have solved the mystery of marriage. Your illustration of Godly love for your fiancé/fiancée or spouse will explain that you have grasped the meaning of being one with your companion.

The most practical analogy of marriage planning would be home building. Building a home and building a marriage are both processes that turn out successful when built according to certified plans or blueprints. Both are certain when they are prepared by the book and built with codes in place. And both are proven when development is taken slow and is not hurried.

If your plans are to build a relationship that will stand the test of time, be sure to follow plans where God is the architect and master builder. Follow the process in sequence while avoiding the temptation to rush or do steps out of order. Build "your" ideal home one day at a time. Put the dedication and effort into the building process. Never get frustrated if your home does not look like your parent's home, your neighbor's home, or the house down the street. And be sure to not get discouraged when your home does not initially resemble the picture you saw in a book. Your marriage can look the same or better over time if you put in the hard work and dedication necessary.

The keys to building your ideal home are:

- The Blueprint
- The Materials

"MARRIAGE PLANS FOR TWO" (MP42)

− The Workforce (Craftsmen and Craftswomen)

A blueprint is a detailed visual plan or course of action that serves as a model for your course of action. The blueprint must be reviewed by the entity that will grant a permit to build and inspect the building process (God and his Word for a Christian Marriage).

Materials are the elements or items from which something is made. The items are specified on the plans/blueprints for building your ideal home. Be sure to include biblical items such as Communication, Wisdom, Love, Commitment, Sacrifice, Trust, Honor, Intimacy, etc. when building a happy marriage.

Craftsmanship is the ability of a skilled and knowledgeable workforce to make or produce what is drawn on the blueprint. You and your fiancé/spouse have the duty to be the trained personnel who should possess an acquired awareness and the ability to build a successful home and marriage.

Good plans, materials, and tools alone do not mean anything if the craftsmen do not know the proper way to use them. Therefore, couples must keep checking the marriage they are trying to build against the blueprint, items, and devices in their possession. The more education and training they have usually determined how successful they will become. The couple then must apply how much they know against what they are trying to build.

Substandard goods may cause problems later in the building process, so do not use them. Quality products and finishes cost more initially, but the upfront sacrifice will add value to your marriage and last longer.

The plans should be reviewed before work begins to ensure the standards, specifications, structure, and support are adequate for what the couple is trying to build and where they are building it. The location is also very important, as the home should be built on "a solid rock." Once approved, the overseer uses the building plans as a guide during the inspection process to ensure the workforce/couple are following the plans set forward as they achieve their building milestones.

The "MARRIAGE PLANS FOR TWO" concept is designed by God and if he is your appointed architect and inspector, he will help you examine yourself and your ongoing relationship to make sure your house becomes a home.

On most homes, the foundation that supports the building is rarely seen by others, but it is the most important component of the building. It usually takes about 20% of the time and finances but is well worth it if formed and set correctly. It will support and withstand all the internal and external loads the building will experience over its lifetime. And like all marriages, the deeper and more solid the foundation, the more stories that can be added to the structure. Present foresight and wisdom prepare you both for events, planned and unplanned, in the future. If your marriage is built on Jesus' principles, then your marriage can stand and withstand the strongest winds and storms that may come your way to adversely affect your relationship.

So, when you begin your "MARRIAGE PLANS FOR TWO," be sure to have the right strategies, resources, and a mind to work until the end. And again, when your house is not turning into your ideal home, be sure to check and see if both of you are following the blueprints. The Word of God does not return void.

When your home is built, remember to keep the original plans because it is best to have them when you want or need to do an addition to the existing structure. Changes are a part of life and most certainly a part of marriage. Anticipate changes and make preparation for modifications before they come.

Work for the heart of your fiancé/spouse and save plenty of love. Love pays the emotional bills and provides the protection and security needed to keep a relationship safe. Love is the power that keeps the romantic lights on and fire burning. Love does not wait until the relationship is falling apart before fixing it. Love foresees the needs of the relationship and listens to their spouse's desire to do what it takes to keep the house a happy home. Love in a happy home is a conduct of action that a person chooses to act on and decides to carry out because they value the person, they decided to spend the rest of their lives with.

God will always uphold a marriage that follows his plans and specifications. He has a method in place for a couple to work together and stay together after their *career plans* end in retirement, and their *family plans* see their last child leave home. It is called "MARRIAGE PLANS FOR TWO."

*The mystery of marriage is the unification of
two individuals becoming one cohesive unit
that is loyal to one another.*

CHAPTER 2

THE SEVEN STAGES

The dynamics of a marriage relationship differs from one couple to another. To some, it is love at first sight, while for others, love grows over time. Some couples may have met before they graduated high school and stayed in a committed relationship for years until they decided to get married. While others may have been introduced by friends, family, or met at work and eventually got married. Then there are those who fit somewhere in between the two. But everyone has their own love story to tell, and those stories may have some similarities in the narrative.

The purpose of this "MARRIAGE PLANS FOR TWO" handbook is to prepare you for the next chapter in your relationship process. It should also inspire you to set in motion the composition of subsequent chapters as you navigate through the various states that may lead to marriage. When you consider the fact that no two people are 100% alike, you will see that it is unlikely that all relationships or marriages will be 100% alike. And when compared, no two stories will be exactly the same. For that reason, everyone must take the time to study, get to know, and carefully examine and analyze the person they are interested in marrying. Getting along may be simple most of the time, but no one ever said that it is or will be easy. A **constructive** marriage is simply two imperfect people, from two totally different backgrounds, with two different sets of traditions, and two different minds and personalities, trying to accomplish a rhythm that will allow two different hearts to beat as one. Blending two hearts into one is not impossible if good planning and preparation are part of the process. First you must agree to the "MARRIAGE PLANS FOR TWO" concept for your lives. Once in agreement with your ideas, it will take both of you to agree to keeping your commitment to one another to carry out those plans.

You must set out on a quest for knowledge to learn each other's traits, characteristics, and cultures to determine if the two of you are compatible. Most importantly, you will need to know if the two of you can co-exist together and live happily ever after. You will also want to commit to bringing out the best version of your partner and never allowing them to deteriorate because of taking marriage vows.

There is a major difference between finding someone who is compatible and someone who is enjoyable. An enjoyable person is someone another person can have fun or a good time with. A person that is entertaining and provides a season of pleasure or satisfaction. They are basically someone to enjoy the benefits of a shallow relationship with because the focus is on what pleases the individual in the short term, rather than what suits both individuals' long term. While an enjoyable person is good for a happy marriage, the marital relationship is limited if that person is not also compatible.

Compatibility goes beyond being one hundred percent alike and weighs heavily on the ability of how able a couple is to operate in harmony together (an intertwining of two people's lives into one). It encompasses how well two people will work together with minimum modifications or qualms. It is very important to the success of the marriage if each person can be themselves (personality, mannerisms, etc.) and not have to pretend, perform, or profess to be someone they are not comfortable being. If a person willfully chooses to change areas of their lives just to be with someone else, then so be it. Unfortunately, if they are not able to keep up the façade, they may never truly be happy.

No one should ever enter a relationship thinking that they can change their fiancé/spouse either before or after they marry them. It is merely impossible. It is okay to note that some people will change their own behavior for someone that they truly love, but an individual will never "change" a person that does not want to change themselves. The wedding altar is a place of commitment and not a place of transformation. The person that is standing at the altar is who you will marry. Saying "I do" will not change selfishness, meanness, frugalness, stinginess, passiveness, laziness, etc.

Therefore, it is important to learn everything about someone while they are single and not married to you. Attempting to persuade or influence your partner's behaviors after marrying them may be to your own detriment. Again, interpersonal change is a choice that can only be made by the individual themselves.

One can enhance their relationship and assist their cause by communicating their preferences and knowing what pleases the one they are trying to build a relationship with. But never should someone try to force or make someone be what they are not or chooses not to be. In marriage, they will only frustrate themselves in trying.

It is counterproductive for a person to lower their standards and try to force a relationship. You should never compromise on your core values and beliefs. It is impossible to escape from your conscience when trying to pretend what is wrong is right or knowing that what they settle for will not make them happy. Couples must remember that others may have to deal with your bad choice, but an ill-advised marriage causes you to live with your bad choice.

God designed marriage to be a good thing, a pleasurable experience, and a benefit that enhances the lives of both parties involved. He says in his word that when a man finds a wife, he finds a "good thing" and obtains favor from the Lord (Proverbs 18:22).

As Lisa and I delved deeper into the marriage progression we realized that the educational focus should happen before marriage instead of expending time on extensive marital counseling after the wedding.

After careful consideration, we decided to separate each stage of a relationship to allow for a better understanding of how relationships start from its infancy and grows as couples travel through each stage. If a couple chooses to make "MARRIAGE PLANS FOR TWO," they should ultimately end up, living the "happily ever after" stage of "Real Love."

Each stage plays an important part in a couple's marriage journey. The seven stages of maturation in relationships before and after the wedding are listed below.

1. Informal
2. Friendship
3. In-Love
4. Courtship
5. Reality
6. Focused Love
7. Real Love

Each stage has a distinguishable characteristic or developmental period in the relationship. The amount of time to transition from one phase to another and the exact sequence will vary from couple to couple. To fully enjoy the true meaning and intention of marriage, everyone must become mature and responsible to attain stage seven (Real Love). This can occur either before or after the wedding.

> 1. *The Informal Relationship* - *(Unplanned, infrequent, and informal communications occur. These occurrences usually take place by happenstance, and conversations should include information related to everyday life events, news stories, or business dealings. These interactions usually take place when they meet in traditional or public settings and*

should be brief in nature. It is important to note that neither party is seeking a relationship during this stage.

The Informal Relationship is basically someone that a person is not familiar with and may have casual contact or social exchange. They may see the other person at work, school, the gym, coffee shop, etc. They may casually speak on infrequent intervals with no personal conversations held during the informal relationship stage.

2. *<u>The Recognized Friendship</u> - (The two individuals are communicating on purpose, with a specific end goal of becoming friends. These interactions include only the individuals that each feels free to be their authentic selves around; individuals who they support and are supported by; and individuals that they can be open with and trust without fear of their confidentiality being betrayed).*

The Recognized Friendship is someone that a person chooses to become familiar with and enter a formal friendship by personal choice. A formal acquaintance or relationship is one where two individuals gain knowledge of one another's personality traits, character, culture, what is acceptable, and most importantly, learn about each other's core values. During this state of the relationship, open communication takes place about future goals as well as past successes, failures, or shortcomings. The individuals also spend lots of quality time together to help them determine whether they are compatible. This is where they either choose to remain friends or to consider one another as a suitable mate for marriage.

3. *In-Love* - *(Caring and calculated communications take place about pleasures, happiness, future dreams, and the things that fulfill each individual. Some people temporarily substitute reality with emotions and role play instead of totally being forthright and transparent).*

IN-LOVE is an affection or adoration that causes a strong emotional desire to want to be with the person of interest intensely in the beginning. Over time these feelings may fluctuate as (or if) the fascination wears off or the intensity lessens.

Some call being in-love a form of infatuation or an obsession because it is a biological response that is initiated by an individual's personal perceived preferences and can be triggered by one, or a combination of the five senses (sight, smell, taste, touch, or hearing). A person can be in-love with the other person's fame, beauty, eye color, voice, physical shape, sense of humor, wealth, personality, etc. without even knowing the true person.

A person who is in the in-love stage is usually driven by their emotions instead of analyzing truths and recognizing and reacting to their partner's flaws. Their focus is typically on what's going on in the moment, instead of focusing on the future because they are experiencing a moderate or major void of reality. This often misleads one to only view the good traits that a person possesses, while overlooking the facts that are exhibited by their behavior. You can easily say that many people in the In-Love stage may be irrational and blind.

Pastor Allmon enjoyed telling the story of a man who fell in-love with an opera singer. She was beautiful in every way. She had long hair, green eyes, unblemished skin, and a shapely body. They eventually married and as she began to undress on the honeymoon night, it was then, and only then that the man began to second guess his decision in marrying the opera singer. When she pulled off her wig, took her green contact lenses out, got rid of the foundation that covered her facial blemishes, wiped off the pretty pink coloring from her lips, removed her fake hips, fake buttocks, and fake leg, his jaw dropped, and he was left speechless. When she asked him if he was still in-love? his reply was "sing baby sing."

Being in-love can be as pleasant as it is dangerous because a person can be so intoxicated with, or be in a drunken love, where soundness of mind and lack of good judgement are sometimes compromised. It is often said that "people who are in this stage tend to do and say things that they would not ordinarily do or say while sober." When a person is inebriated by love, or toxic, they often cannot eat, nor sleep. Feelings of inadequacy may materialize due to over-thinking about who they are in-love with.

The intoxicated in-love state can be impacted as the couple realizes there is a crossover point where the bliss wears off, the fantasy and the imaginary high of the relationship ends and reality sets in. This happens over time as the couple really gets to know each other better.

Their true attitudes, ambitions, habits, morals, etc. are discovered as the two spend added scheduled time together. The advantages, sacrifices or disadvantages become noticeable.

The high does not have to end when the potentials and limitations are recognized if both parties decide to truly love each other as is (exactly how they see each other). Once the blinders are removed, continuing the relationship must be intentional from that point forward. But beware, there is the possibility that one can fall in-love by themselves, for their self, and for selfish reasons. For example, one person may be in love with the idea of being in love. They may actually think that the love is "Real Love" when in fact, it is only a romantic obsession.

Contrary to popular belief, sex is a very powerful act. Once a person freely gives their body in a sexual relationship, they are connecting themselves to their sexual partner for a lifetime due to an associated soul tie. Some lovers do not realize the influential connection they made in the soul tie, while others hope that the connection will somehow magically attach them to a lasting relationship with their partner. But soul ties do not always bond a relationship and sustain happiness through time. It sometimes does the opposite and works against the individual by causing deep anguish and regret for many years to come.

Always be open to hearing and valuing the advice of your true friends and family. It may be difficult at first, but at least listen to what they have to say. Take the time to ponder their suggestions and really consider their comments when you are in-love. Do not have a "tell me what I want to hear" attitude and a pessimistic reaction to their advice. Years later, when the early days of the in-love excitement wears off, those words may come to mind.

Being in-love is an awesome feeling! It is an awesome place to be in with the right person. When you are making forever decisions allow yourself some time to move past the newness of the in-love state. Let the in-love experience run its course so that you can have a clear view of the other person and get the opportunity to see that person for who they really are. Some people are great at putting on a front, but they can only pretend for a season before their actual character is revealed.

It is a gamble to marry someone before you see their true colors and experience genuine love. Take the time to evaluate the risks and rewards before you make a lifetime investment.

A person in-love may only see the newness of the relationship and the excitement of what the other person said and did. They may be so locked in the game of anticipating the next meeting, that they may only see what they want to see instead of looking at the whole relationship, inside and out. They can inadvertently see the advantages without even looking at the sacrifices or disadvantages.

Some people may ignore small signs and signals while dating. But once married, those small signs and signals can turn into super-sized irritations that can cause divisions between the two.

The infatuation may be lust that is dressed in love clothing. Realtors do not recommend buying a house on looks on the outside alone. They recommend a showing on the inside; an appraisal to determine net worth, equity and future value, property history and a title search to make sure the house is clear prior to purchase. Lisa and I suggest you take the same approach, before marriage, when offering to obtain the heart of someone you believe you love.

Doing the right thing at the right time is more productive than the right thing at the wrong time, the wrong thing at the right time and especially the wrong thing at the wrong time. Timing is important. Especially when considering marriage.

At the end of the day, you want to live with the fruit of good decisions instead of living with the regrets of bad decisions. Do not make hasty decisions without contemplating the consequences. Use the dating period wisely to weigh out the consequences. True love will wait, but lust will not.

> 4. *Courtship (Dating and Engagement)* - *(Honest and transparent communications take place about future expectations, goals, and family values as both individuals search for affirmations to verify if the two of them are compatible).*
>
> **Courtship (Dating and Engagement)** is a process designed for discovery. In this stage two people voluntarily enter a more serious friendship and will engage in more frequent social activities and discussions leading to marriage.

This is the mid-point of the relationship and is also a pivotal point.

Courting and dating can mean the same thing to some people and different things to other people. To most, they are romantic appointments designed to learn more about each other. This stage should be an expedition with good intentions to seek alliance to further grow the common interest with a friend.

Engagement is a pledge for exclusiveness in the relationship where the couple makes a promise to be involved and affiliated with each other (only) to determine further compatibility before they marry. As a prelude to marriage, the engagement should be respected by both entities as a commitment stage before they share a home and enter a more intimate relationship with one another.

I Timothy 5:1-2 admonishes that males should treat all the females in the church as mothers or sisters, and that females should treat all males in the church as fathers or brothers. With a pure mind.

When there is a shift in the atmosphere and someone of the opposite sex is viewed differently than a brother or sister, and an interest to enter a relationship is considered, then it should be communicated openly. If the interest is reciprocated it should then lead to dating, courting, engagement and hopefully marriage.

Like any formal education, you must invest the time to gain the knowledge and understanding of you and your perspective spouse. Past public informal environments are good talking points to gauge present values.

Personality traits are forever. You were born with yours and so was your potential spouse. Each personality type has their advantages, but they also come with associated sacrifices. Love languages, like personalities, are unique individual traits that you should learn if you want to be able to effectively communicate with the person you have interest in.

To obtain a complete compatibility check, each person must be transparent with the other; be real with one another; and both must use wisdom during this stage. A truthful and sincere pledge of allegiance, with no guile or dishonesty, should be present in this phase of the relationship.

To build trust and be trusted, genuineness must start in the courtship. It will be vital to discuss some personal details or experiences (good and bad) with your projected spouse at some point in the process. Remember, be sure not to tell it all on the first date.

Unless someone with high credibility can vouch for the character of an individual, we always recommend that you have been friends with a person for at least two years and in an involved or close friendship at least one of those years before marriage. If both parties are validated, a yearlong enhanced friendship/courtship may suffice. Most of the time it is usually easier when you marry a friend than a stranger because you have invested the time and energy into building a trusting relationship. This allows you to have a better idea of the real person that you are choosing to spend your life with.

One should never let desperation set in before reality sets in. Never overlook a person's faults to fulfill your need to be involved in a relationship.

Keep in mind, when attempting to finalize a courtship or engagement, the perspective mate is at the top of their game and on their best behavior. They strive to be who and what their fiancé/fiancée wants them to be. During this time, they are exhibiting and showing evidence of what and who they have the potential to become. So, do not fool yourself into thinking that this display will become the norm. Take your time and make sure you see the person for who they really are and what your relationship will be like once you say I do.

Make sure that you get to know their family and friends. Keep in mind that their family is usually on their best behavior when they meet you. Use this time to determine if your spouse will have trouble separating from their family and cleaving to you. Test whether you may have to set boundaries that could cause division between the two of you. If possible, meet their ex-friends and find out reasons why previous relationships did not work.

Anyone can choose to make changes and get better over time. The questions you must ask yourself in the present are: What amount of time is necessary for the change to take place? How long are you willing to wait? Do you wait for them to change before or after you get married? It is better to wait until you are sure you are compatible with the right person than to rush into a relationship and marry the wrong person.

The goal is to marry the spouse that is designed for you and not a person who is designed for someone else. You should never convince yourself to hurry when making any important decisions when you have the option to take your time. You should never commit your life to marriage based on promises, potential, financial gain, loneliness, sex, feelings, excitement, emotions or because others think that you all make a good couple. Entering marriage at this point should be a choice and not a compulsion or an obligation.

> 5. <u>*REALITY*</u> *- (True and transparent communications take place about expected responsibilities, personality differences, acceptable values and core values as genuine expectations begin to manifest themselves).*
>
> **REALITY** is a point or season in the relationship where the real "you" is discovered by the one you are in a relationship with.

Your spouse or spouse-to-be now sees their companion for who they are, always was, and possibly always will be. As a person gets comfortable with someone in that person's environment, they will relax and be transparently themselves. And as they become casual, they easily reveal their true character and heart.

As the prospective spouse begins to relax, the other person must be real with themselves as agendas, intentions and motives become more visible. They must decide whether these traits and characteristics align with their own or if they are willing to continue a relationship based on these revelations.

God created everyone with a distinct spirit, soul, and body so you do not have to put on, or step outside of your true character to please someone else. You can be yourself, and this will let the other person know who you truly are before they say I do.

Always remember to keep your identity when in a relationship. Your uniqueness is what separates you from everyone else. The person that is in a relationship with you should choose you because of who you genuinely are. They should not intend for you to become who they are or require you to change to be with them.

And if a person morphs into someone they are not for the sake of a relationship, it will only make them miserable. Two people can be different and happy together. It is better to reach this level of reality in a relationship before marriage. You want to find the authentic person. You want to see them at their worst as well as their best because marriage will bring tests that will bring out an assortment of emotions, feelings, characteristics, and behaviors in an individual.

Many divorces have taken place because women thought they were marrying Dr. Jekyll but did not know he was also Mr. Hyde. A host of men thought they had found an educated and beautiful flower named Ms. Isley only to be subdued by Poison Ivy. On the other hand, many women married Clark Kent and later found out that he was Superman. A score of men thought they hit the jackpot when they married Princess Dianna only to find out that she exceeded their expectations when they found out she was Wonder Woman also.

Either way, the reality of marriage is real and not make believe. Marriage is for mature adults. It is not for little boys and girls in adult sized bodies. The trials of marriage can be overwhelming if you are not prepared. If "MARRIAGE PLANS FOR TWO" are not made beforehand, tests and trials can set back the childish and cause them to run back home to their parents due to their immaturity.

6. FOCUSED PURPOSE - *(Conscientious and comprehensive communications take place about commitment, unity, sacrifices, and challenges as each person agrees to extend the courtship/marriage).*

FOCUSED PURPOSE is when an individual deliberately strengthens their own personal shortcomings and weakness in preparation of becoming one with their spouse to solidify their relationship and unity.

The responsibility of everyone is to work on themselves first and their spouse secondly, if necessary. The Bible teaches that you must get the beam out of your eye before you attempt to get the mote (splinter) out of someone else's eye. Good marriages are developed intentionally and on purpose.

The commitment begins at the courtship stage for you to obtain the necessary information about marriage and the person you are interested in marrying. Both parties must intentionally study the personality and love language of their perspective partner to willfully accommodate their needs and wants (sometimes before your own if you really love them). Both individuals must be willing to sacrifice to make the other person happy. The relationship cannot be one-sided if you want to have a sustainable and successful marriage.

You must deliberately evaluate where the relationship has come from, its current state, and what needs to be done to enter or continue a successful, romantic, and lifelong marriage.

Communication is key!!! You must communicate openly and honestly, and as often as possible with your intended spouse.

Communication is not an option in a marriage; it is a necessity if the river of love is to continually flow. If you stop communicating, the river will sit still. Still water becomes stagnant and will eventually dry up.

If someone can fall in love, make no mistake, they can also fall out of love. If someone can find love, then they also can lose it. If love can increase than it can also decrease, and if love can grow it can also wither.

Where there is no wood (Focused Purpose) the fire (Love, passion, adventure) goes out.

> 7. <u>**GENUINE LOVE**</u> - *(Thorough and thoughtful communications take place about genuine feelings, personal stances, transparent point of views, pure thoughts, valid concerns, and behaviors).*
>
> **GENUINE LOVE** is an authentic feeling of concern and affection that has developed over time and is meant to surpass time.

It transcends their personality, flaws, bodily presence, and differences. An individual willfully chooses to commit to another based on knowledge, truth, feelings, and logical reasoning.

They intentionally fulfill the other person's needs to be loved without looking for any compensation in return. They carry out a forever decision because they genuinely love the person to which they are committing.

To marry at this point is a well-chosen declaration to a carefully selected individual. A lifetime pronouncement to be lived one day at a time. The dedication must span the space of time because maturity brings about changes.

A word from the wise, to the wise. Before marriage, everyone that feels a connection with someone should beware of the flesh. You want to spend time with your spouse to be, but you do not want to do anything at the expense of your relationship with God. Therefore, the amount of time that you spend together should be predicated on whether or not your flesh is kept in check or not.

Lisa and I were both very devout Christians when we got engaged. We were also very young. One thing for sure was we really wanted to be saved and stay in the will of God. But when we took the step to be more than just friends and began to spend more time together something humanly and natural happened. Feelings for intimacy would come upon us unexpectedly. The more time we spent together, the greater and more frequent the temptation. Our love for God was so genuine and that made those feeling so much more perplexing. It was not intentional; it was not wanted, and neither one of us desired to jeopardize our relationship with God. The feelings or emotions were not cravings or yearnings, but more of a spontaneous reaction. We talked about them, prayed about them, and sought to fix them to no avail.

Finally, I decided to talk with our pastor to find out what was wrong with us (lol). His guidance was truly enlightening. He said it was important to recognize the enemy and know your limitations. He explained that although it is important to spend time with the individual you plan on marrying, it is more important to stay the course, and do it according to the instructions in the scriptures.

He commended us for not acting on the temptation but warned that seductive spirts can lure you into a trap that the enemy sets to separate us from our vow to remain true to God. The Bible admonishes you to submit yourselves to God, resist the devil and he will flee from you in every area except sexual sins. The Bible instructs in I Corinthians 6:18 and II Timothy 2:22 to "Flee fornication…." and "Flee also youthful lust…..," respectfully. Lisa and I took those scriptures seriously.

Therefore, our Pastor's advice was to spend a modest amount of time together. If either of you felt tempted, then it would be best to leave and talk on the phone to avoid intimate traps. He advised us to spend more time in group settings to avoid enticement. His instructions guided us to not fight the flesh. He said it would only subject us to the guilt and condemnation that could overwhelm us. He further instructed us, most of all, to pray. He told us that our goal should be to set a good example for the other young couples coming behind.

Through all of this, we learned that "Genuine Love" is real love and if someone truly loves you, they will always want only the best for you. Genuine Love is selfless, it is unconditional, and it is always giving. Genuine Love is not diminished by time, nor weakened by circumstances. True love comes from and is manifested from within. You cannot hide it and dare not divide it. Find Genuine Love and you will live happily ever after.

*Genuine Love is selfless, it is unconditional,
and it is always giving.*

CHAPTER 3

FOUNDATIONS – THE PROLOGUE

After working in marriage ministry for quite some time, Lisa and I began discussing what would be the best illustration to show couples what it takes to build a happy and successful marriage. As we brainstormed many ideas came to mind.

Because Lisa is an audiovisual person that comprehends information, and I am a visual person that conceptualizes by logic we had to agree on a format from which we could teach from pictures and diagrams so that all parties involved are able to visualize the associated information.

We had previously used word games and fill in the blanks for ice breakers, but it all came together with the creation of the chart illustrated on the following page. The chart is comprised of different sized foundations which were stacked one upon another and held together with a common bonding agent. These foundations were steps that led up to a house sitting on top with an older couple standing in front of their happy home, waving together. The goal stated is: "Build Your Marriage On A Solid Foundation.

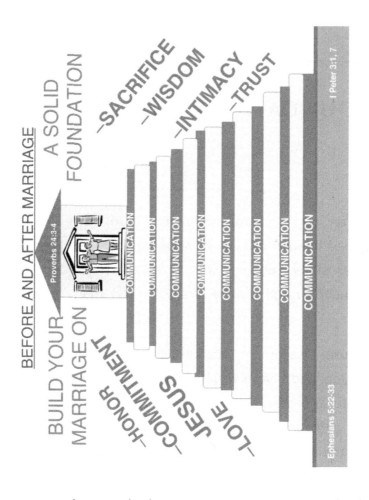

There were nine words that were common among the various speakers at the marriage seminars we had attended over the years: Communication, Wisdom, Love, Commitment, Sacrifice, Trust, Honor, Intimacy, and in all the Christian seminars - Jesus.

The challenge we present to the couples is to assign each foundation a word from the bottom to the top with the bottom being "extremely important" and the top being "very important," in relation to building a happy home. Then, compare answers and discuss the reasoning behind the decisions made.

Lisa and I must admit that most of our answers differed in our initial trial run. But after exchanging viewpoints and coming to a meeting of minds we finally agreed on an order acceptable to both of us. A few days later we began to get phone calls and invitations to come and speak at married and couples' events. In preparation, we began to dig deeper into the chart and attended more Christian seminars both online and in person. We realized that we needed to make some modifications to the chart. We decided the bottom foundation (Jesus), and bonding agent (communication) were non-negotiables. Jesus is always the right answer for Christian marriages and should be the sub-surface, or underlying foundation to uphold all loving relationships. Communication, as we will see, is the glue or bonding agent that holds any type of relationship together, Secular or Spiritual.

We originally had love before wisdom only to find out that the principal component of bonded relationships is wisdom when it comes to making "MARRIAGE PLANS FOR TWO." The following page is the order we decided on. Let us start with explaining communication in the next chapter and continue with the rest.

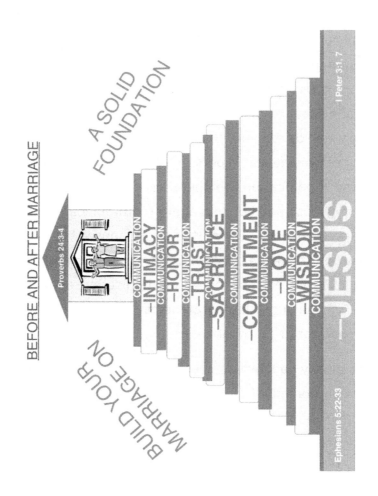

CHAPTER 4

FOUNDATIONS - COMMUNICATION

Communication is not a foundation, but it is a building component in the marriage structure that cannot be understated. It is the bonding agent that stabilizes, connects, and holds together the participants to keep the union by collaboration.

We allowed it to be a given in the chart to emphasize the importance of communication throughout the relationship (before and after the wedding). Communication should never get old or outdated. Couples will need it just as much in the middle as they do at the beginning and latter, golden years of marriage.

The dictionary defines communication as:

   1. A process by which information is exchanged between individuals through a common system of symbols signs or behavior;

   2. Personnel engaged in transmitting or exchanging information;

   3. A technique for expressing ideas effectively (as in speech);

4. A method to transmit information, thought, or feeling so that it is satisfactorily received or understood.

It is crucial to the health of the relationship that couples communicate about everything, all the time. And everything means everything. The goal is for the sender/speaker to effectively transmit the message to the receiver/listener in a manner that they understand and willfully accept it.

This can lead to personable communication where one spouse interacts with their spouse in a way that they feel loved and understood. But this level of communication can only be accomplished by taking the time to find out how their spouse's mind works and then engaging their interests.

Each spouse must do whatever it takes to realistically exchange, share, and receive messages with their spouse. Both must be good listeners, but only one can talk, speak, converse, commune, signal, or sign at a time.

If one spouse comprehends what the other spouse is trying to communicate it is an effective exchange of information. If one spouse does not understand what the other spouse is trying to communicate it is miscommunication. If one spouse does not want to hear what the other spouse is trying to say they can block the transmission. Blocking transmissions can be the result when one spouse does not want to deal with or respond to a disagreeable or unlikable subject or situation.

Either way, continuous failures to communicate can lead married couples to dangers expressed below:

- They cannot meet each other's physical needs.
- They cannot meet each other's emotional needs.
- They cannot meet each other's spiritual needs.
- They cannot resolve differences.
- They cannot encourage one another.
- They will fail in learning to know and understand each other.
- Emotional wounds will stay open and not heal.

Effective and proper communication will always be necessary and useful. Couples must make time to talk and then talk. They must make time to listen and then listen. They then must process the communications and respond. One side of communication is knowing how and when to talk. The other side of communication is knowing how to listen.

There should not be a subject where a married couple cannot have an open and honest conversation about. Sometimes it will be necessary to have the serious conversations and dive into the issue at hand without being judgmental, critical, or irrational.

When in doubt, each couple should have the liberty to ask instead of making the mistake of communication by assumption. Mind reading is a power that 99.9% of couples do not have. One should never assume their spouse knows what they are thinking or feeling. Communication can put one another's minds at ease through properly interacting with one another. Both parties can eliminate insecurities by not letting assumptions in their minds grow into obstacles.

All couples will experience differences or have disagreements. Differences and disagreements are inevitable in marriage. It is not if they will happen, instead, it is when they will happen. When you both sit down and finish discussing the "why" questions, be sure to address the "how" solutions. How do we do better and how do we avoid the same thing from happening again? People that love each other differ in opinions sometimes. Some disparities will be obvious and others unapparent.

These lack of "meeting of minds" must be handled with maturity and the couple will learn and practice "safe arguing." Watch what you say, how you say it, where you say it , and who you say it in front of. Respect yourself, respect your spouse and do not argue angry. Avoid bringing up past issues. Constantly referencing past issues indicates that the issue is still unresolved. Also, be sure to call your spouse by their name.

The devil is crafty and constantly entices bad communication and intercepts good communication. He sometimes causes one spouse to ignore the other and at other times replaces the good communication with perceived differences that causes misunderstandings and arguments.

But the certainty is, unless there is communication there will be problems. And no one can fix a problem if they do not know there is a problem and what that problem is. You cannot mend spiritual needs or encourage one another without properly communicating in some way or another. Daily communication is critical to avoiding unnecessary quarrels. If your spouse enters "Survival Mode" and senses a need to defend or protect themselves by any means necessary, all clear communication will be inhibited.

Physical and emotional needs are biological and can affect one's thinking and behaviors. Just as food, water, sleep, and exercise are necessary to maintain the performance of a physical body in a marriage; belonging, security and the peace of knowing that one's spouse will always be there for them are necessary for the mental well-being of a person.

Heart to heart conversations about enjoyable, regretful, and imperfect actions or situations are beneficial when handled properly and should never be avoided if you are to have a healthy marriage. It is not if you communicate, it is when you communicate. It is not when you communicate, but how you communicate.

The more one spouse makes their husband/wife feel accepted, the less chance that insecurities arise. Eventually, it allows those who have self-doubt to take down the walls that can involuntarily or unconsciously separate them from their spouse due to fear of rejection.

Therefore, each spouse must also learn to verbalize their appreciation for their husband/wife and acknowledge the positive contributions they bring to the relationship to counter any low self-esteem or doubt of their importance. If each spouse can be real with themselves and take the time to learn more about themselves and their spouse, it will make it easier to express themselves and be real with their spouse. Simply put, unmet physical needs can lead to emotional issues and unmet emotional needs can lead to physical issues.

Because marriage is an event sometimes full of experimental experiences as time goes on, knowing how to communicate your needs to your spouse daily enables your marriage to grow and blossom as you are provided with knowledge, understanding, and wisdom. It is hard for some people's heart to understand what their eyes cannot see, and their ears cannot hear. So, express and verbalize yourself in a positive way. Your relationship can get better over time if good communication is prevalent.

Each spouse will have days when they get it all right and other days when they fall short of what is expected. Sometimes you can express words that either heal or cause hurt. Mentally, upsetting actions can cut deep and cause open emotional wounds to the offended spouse. A speaker once said, "a six-inch tongue can tear down a six-foot person."

Although painful, wounds can heal over time with proper treatment, but cannot mend if they are continually reopened or picked at. If emotional wounds are to heal, there must be forgiveness. Contrary to popular belief, because every deep wound leaves a scar, it will not be forgotten. There is no such thing as forgive and forget. But with proper communication, both parties can forgive and move forward, overcome, and rebuild from any injury incurred.

If a couple is serious about making their marriage work, they must make their love and actions count by communicating openly and effectively. They must learn to adjust to the unconscious imperfections of their spouse. They must learn to look and listen, to know and understand the "Right There" or "That's It" expressions. If you have ever had a bad itch or ache in a place where you could not reach and you had to get help from your spouse to scratch or massage the right spot, then you understand what we are saying. You give good directions ("up, up, a little more, to the left, right there, that is it. Ooohh, Aaahh").

The same principle applies when your spouse is working with you to please you and give you the maximum pleasure, relief, or benefits in all other areas associated with marriage. Communication is your ally.

There should not be a subject where married couples cannot have an open and honest conversation about.

CHAPTER 5

FOUNDATIONS - WISDOM

Proverbs 24:3-4(KJV):

1. Through wisdom is an house builded; and by understanding it is established.
2. And by knowledge shall the chambers be filled with all precious and pleasant riches

Proverbs 24:3-4 (AMP):

1. Through [skillful and godly] wisdom a house [a life, a home, a family] is built, and by understanding it is established [on a sound and good foundation].
2. And by knowledge its rooms are filled with all precious and pleasant riches.

Wise decisions are necessary in every phase of a building project. The type of project is irrelevant (house, home, office, family, tower, or marriage). The concepts from start to finish are the same.

Wisdom is the principal thing and ensures that marriages begin right and endure the storms of life as the couple sticks together. Instruction creates in each spouse's mind, an image of what the couple must envision and receive to understand marriage. Knowledge makes the process, and finished product, more precious and pleasant. The knowledge each spouse learned about achieving a quality marriage will be put into action so their home can be a happy place. Understanding establishes a marriage and makes a house a home. When there is understanding in a marriage the husband wants to be on the inside of the house with his wife instead of on top of the roof in the corner, and the wife wants to be at home with her husband instead of making excuses to find somewhere else to go. And over time, discretion assists couples to do the right thing, at the right time and for the right purpose. Both strive to do better because they know better as they apply wisdom and discretion.

God, in his infinite wisdom, provided believers with the book of Proverbs. If you choose to dig deeper for spiritual awareness, this book of Wisdom will provide insight on how to live life skillfully. It is a divine point of view to assist all mankind by providing specific models of how each person can live practical lives and maximize their relationships while emulating God's proposed actions and expectations.

From Proverbs 1:2-7 we extracted a five-step concept which we call *"Proverbs: Countdown To Success"*.

FOUNDATIONS - WISDOM

Proverbs 1:2-7 (KJV):

1. To know wisdom and instruction; to perceive the words of understanding;
2. To receive the instruction of wisdom, justice, and judgement, and equity;
3. To give subtility to the simple, to the young man knowledge and discretion.
4. A wise man will hear, and will increase learning; and a man of understanding shall attain unto wise counsels;
5. To understand a proverb, and the interpretation; the words of the wise, and their dark sayings.
6. The fear of the Lord is the beginning of knowledge: but fools despise wisdom and instruction.

These five concepts from Proverbs apply to every facet of life; including marriages. So, when you start making "MARRIAGE PLANS FOR TWO" be sure you remember them and use them as the road map to get you to your destination. It will be in your best interest to not start without them. Include them in the preparation of your trip, apply them to get ready for launch, for takeoff, and for protection as you enter new marital stratospheres. Let them sustain you along the journey and let them prepare you for safe landings. These five concepts can take you where your marriage has never gone before. So, let the countdown begin:

➢ 5 - Five Words to Obtain
➢ 4 - Four Phrases of Progression
➢ 3 - Three Classifications of People
➢ 2 - Two Decisions to Choose

- ➢ 1 - One Life to Love
- ➢ BLAST OFF... into a Happy Marriage

Five Words to Obtain

1. Instruction
2. Knowledge
3. Understanding
4. Wisdom
5. Discretion

By studying the definitions, you can see how these five words from Proverbs would be beneficial to you. If you choose to pursue them and embrace them, they will forever change your lives and marriage for the better.

Instruction: the act, process, or art of providing teaching, training, information, advice, knowledge and/or skill to educate and to develop mentally, morally, or aesthetically.

Knowledge: the fact or condition of knowing and retaining something with familiarity gained through or by instruction, awareness, observation and/or experience.

Understanding: a mental comprehension of how to apprehend (perceive, recognize, anticipate or be aware of) actions or environments and arrive at an intelligent conclusion based on acquired knowledge.

Wisdom: the ability to skillfully use knowledge, understanding, discernment and sound judgment to reach wise decisions or just conclusions in dealing with people and situations.

Discretion: an individual's personal choice to exercise good judgement, tact, or prudence in making responsible decisions within their unrestricted power of freedom of choice.

The five words above that you have been asked to obtain are both progressive and intertwined. Progressive because as you receive instruction it opens the door to obtain knowledge. Knowledge opens the door to obtain understanding. Understanding opens the door to obtain wisdom and wisdom opens the door to discretion.

They are intertwined due to the inherent nature of growing in wisdom. The wisdom that each person possesses was initially gained through instructions they obtained. And the wisdom gained can only be maintained in their life if the imparted knowledge and understanding is retained.

But to increase or grow in wisdom, the individual must continually pursue wise instruction to procure additional knowledge and understanding. In other words, one's furtherance of wisdom will be directly proportional to their attainment of the other associated words. The area(s) they have the greatest chance to succeed in will be the area(s) they commit to study and attain.

The more wisdom obtained in the dating process, the more knowledgeable a person will be in noticing what to look for and avoid when choosing a spouse. They better understand what their responsibilities will be and how they should be equipped to fulfill them. The wiser they become, the more discrete they can be and the better choices they will make before and after the wedding.

To plan and build their house [life, home, and family] everyone must set their goals and continually set priorities in obtaining these five words from Proverbs.

If you are serious about your marriage, you will be serious about growing yourself. Growth is measured by increase. As these five words from Proverbs change and expand your life, it will change and expand your relationship and marriage. You must develop your marriage to last for a lifetime. When you grasp the concept of investing in your marriage you will intentionally attend marriage conferences and seminars.

You need instruction to be able to instruct in every area of your relationship and all the marital relationships you will help in your future. You need knowledge to be able to know how to know you and your spouse. The more you know about how your spouse acts, reacts, and thinks will serve you well in bonding throughout your relationship. You need understanding to be able to understand your spouse and all their ways. People do not just wake up one day and decide to be the way they are. There is a story, with a chapter and a verse in their background that explains how they became who they are. It takes wisdom to be wise enough to deal with your spouse in a manner that will keep peace and grow in love. It takes discretion to continually make the right decisions along your marriage adventure.

What good is it to have wisdom and do not use it? Listen to wisdom and you will know where to go, what to do, why you are doing it, and when to make the right moves. You need discretion to make the right choices at the right time. In a marriage, your conduct toward your spouse is the key to an open heart. Integrity starts with discipline and ends with fidelity. You will never have a great marriage if you choose to remain the same or think that you are already there.

Four Phrases of Progression
1. To Know
2. To Perceive
3. To Receive
4. To Give

In Proverbs 1:2-4 we are presented with four hidden gems in plain sight. This continuous and connected series of events are simple but profound. They provide the path of progression from being a student to becoming a teacher.

It is a developmental cycle where you can go from being provided with information (To Know); to seeing exactly what the teacher is trying to get across (To Perceive); to applying what you learned to your own life (To Receive); to advancing the information or teaching what you learned to someone else (To Give). But you can never get from Level One to Level Four unless you choose to become a student of the words you are taught.

To give/share good marriage advice you must receive/apply it to your marriage. To receive/apply marriage advice you must perceive/comprehend what is being communicated. To perceive/comprehend you must know/be taught. How much you know about marriage will open the door for how much you grow in your marriage. How much you grow in your marriage will determine how far you go in your marriage. Marriage is not rocket science, but it is an art you must master if you want success.

To Know:

Proverbs, v.2: "To know wisdom and instruction." To know something, you must either learn it, experience it, or be taught it. Our pastor always emphasized that every verse in the Bible had only one interpretation (original intention), but it could have many applications (uses or analogies for everyday life).

Hosea 4:6 states, "My people are destroyed for lack of knowledge...." When you apply this to marriage you see couples being separated and marriages being destroyed because they either do not have the proper teachings or did not comprehend what they were taught.

When it comes to subjects like love, caring, conflict resolution, money management, forgiveness, etc., some couples do not know enough to do enough. This is due to inexperience and being unprepared before they get married. All couples must be proactive in their quest to make their marriage the best it can be because the Bible holds everyone accountable.

When you know better you can do better. The more someone knows about marriage and how to maintain their marriage, the easier it is to perceive.

To Perceive:

Proverbs v.2 (cont.): "To perceive the words of understanding." To perceive you must see it, comprehend it, or get a revelation of it.

When you understand the process, the dynamics of a marital relationship, yourself, and your spouse or spouse-to-be, the more your mind can become illuminated to God's concept of marriage. Then it becomes easier To Receive.

To Receive:

Proverbs v.3: To receive the instruction of wisdom, justice, and judgement, and equity.

To receive you must be willing to accept, consume, respond, and apply the acquired information, instructions, or experiences.

You may not even agree with the information or instructions sometimes. You may think it is unfair, not right, or inequitable. But, when you acknowledge it as true or the truth, (good or reasonable), you see it for what it is and get better, get up, or get going. To receive denotes you choose not to be mentally blind, deaf, or dumb of facts.

Those who know, perceive, and receive are qualified To Give.

To Give:

Proverbs v.4: To give subtilty to the simple, to the young man knowledge and discretion.

To give instruction, knowledge, understanding and wisdom, a person must first acquire them. Then and only then is that person truly ready to share or teach on a subject.

Wise marriage counsel, instruction, advice, and wisdom is necessary before and throughout marriage. The couple's overall goal is to get what they need to have a successful marriage and progress to phase four, where they can give back to help other couples have successful marriages. It is hard for someone to ever give what they never received. And no one will ever get it if they never search, pursue, find, and hold on to it. Any marriage counsel will not do, it must be in the multitude of wise counsel from wise married couples.

Three Classifications of People

1. Wise People
2. Smart People
3. Fools

It was interesting to find that there was a word that was mentioned more times than four of the five words from Proverbs mentioned above. Fool/Foolish (mentioned 75 times) came in second behind wise/wisdom (mentioned 118 times), and ahead of understand/understanding (mentioned 63 times), knowledge (mentioned 41 times), instruction (mentioned 26 times) and discretion (mentioned 6 times).

Before and after the wedding, both the husband and wife will have to constantly pick a classification as they make decisions in their individual and joined lives. The good thing is that they can only choose a classification for themselves and no one else. Their spouse has his or her own choice to make.

Fortunately, your reputation is not just based on one decision, it is based on the cumulative decisions you have made over time.

The group of decisions frequently made identifies and assigns an individual to one of the three classifications below.

WISE PEOPLE:

Wise people learn from other peoples' accomplishments as well as their mistakes. They pay attention to the details and observe outcomes of others' decisions, actions, etc. and learn what to do and what not to do because they are usually analytical and understand cause and effect.

Take children for example, if you tell them the pot is hot and there are adverse consequences to touching a hot pot they will stand back and repeat your warning that the pot is hot to inform others of the danger and consequences of touching the hot pot although they really do not really know what hot is. But when a curious child, who has been warned, comes along, and touches the hot pot and screams because they have been burned and their hand/finger is blistered, the observing child knows that they not only made the right decision, but also take it to the next level by choosing not to make the same mistake.

Wise spouses take time to learn and make the extra effort to learn from successful as well as unsuccessful marriages to add good sense to their common sense. They learn to open their minds more than they open their mouths and be the right person so they can find and have a good relationship with the right person. Wise people do not get that reputation by mistake. Neither do wise couples.

SMART PEOPLE:

Smart people on the other hand learn from their own accomplishments and mistakes. They are the ones who prefer to find out for themselves and do things their way instead of taking the advice from someone else's words or experiences. Most do not regret their choices until some form of damage is done. They are one portion of the curious kids who touch the pot and burn themselves just to see if what someone said was true. The good thing is they adjust and do not continually make the same mistakes.

But smart people can save themselves a whole lot of heartache, setbacks, inconveniences, and pain if they ever make the decision to take heed to what they hear and see. Experience may be the best teacher, but it is not the best way to learn.

Smart spouses can be very intelligent, witty, and resourceful when they are enthralled in ensuring they are doing everything necessary to make their marriage work. But their curiosity can put them in situations where they make senseless decisions. Their inquisitiveness is rewarding if their course of action goes well, and disastrous if things do not go according to their plan, or, the outcome may fall somewhere between the two.

Many smart spouses find themselves constantly trying to repair their marriages and relationships. But they stand the risk of entering a situation where their spouse feels there are irreconcilable differences; especially if the smart spouse has touched a "hot" pot and got "burned."

FOOLS:

And then there are fools. These are the people who choose not to learn from their own mistakes, other people mistakes and accomplishments, or from life in general.

They are "never learners" because they choose to be. The truth and reality of a lesson is overlooked by foolish people. These are the kids at urgent care or the emergency room every month because they never want to accept that the pot is hot and persist in touching it.

Foolish spouses make the same mistakes repeatedly after promising they would never do it again. They do not learn from the past and bring unwarranted tension into their present marriage due to their selfishness. Fools usually end up either divorced or with unhappy spouses due to their own habitual misdeeds.

The Bible tells us in Proverbs 12:15 (KJV):
'The way of a fool is right in his own eyes: but he that hearkeneth unto counsel is wise.'

Proverbs 18:7 (KJV):
'A fool's mouth is his destruction, and his lips are the snare of his soul.'

Two Decisions to Choose

1. To Hear
2. To Despise

Proverbs 1:5,7 (KJV):
5. 'A <u>wise</u> man will <u>hear</u>, and will increase learning; and a man of understanding shall attain unto wise counsels:
7. The fear of the Lord is the beginning of knowledge: but <u>fools despise</u> wisdom and instruction. '

Every individual and spouse were created as a free moral agent and has the mental capacity to freely choose. Every person falls into one of the following two categories: Those who will hear and obey God's word or those who despise or reject God's word. Each choice comes with a consequence.

The end result you choose for your marriage will depend on the choices you have made up until this point. The Golden Rules in the Word of God works if you have ears to hear. Every answer about life and marriage is in the word of God.

Wise couples use the Word of God as a resource to achieve their silver, gold, and diamond anniversaries. They never stop learning about how to make their marriages better and they never get too old to seek wise counsel. But foolish couples despise wisdom and instruction. Their pride becomes their downfall as they frown on and look down at any marriage, they feel is better than their own.

Proverbs 16:18 (KJV):
'Pride goeth before destruction, and an haughty spirit before a fall.'

God has a lot to say about marriage in His word and each spouse has the right to hear it or despise it. Choose wisely because everyone only has one life to love.

ONE LIFE TO LOVE...

And that brings us to a statement of purpose and truth. Most people say you have one life to live but that is a limited statement. You only have one life to love when it comes to your pursuit of living a full life. What you do with that one life will define who you are.

The question is who you will love with the one life you have. The top three candidates are the three entities where you can become one with: God, yourself, and your spouse. You become one with God when you join yourself to God and allow Him to dwell in you and you willfully abide in Him and endeavor to keep His word. You become one with yourself when you find what makes you happy, relaxed, completed, and self-fulfilled. You become one with your spouse when you take your vows, consummate the marriage, and become one flesh.

As one flesh you are united with your spouse and put your marriage relationship with your spouse above all else. You love them like you love yourself, you protect them, take care of them, provide for them, comfort them, and bring them joy because you voluntarily vowed to be one with your spouse. You find ways to make your spouse love you more and never settle for just a good marriage but keep striving for a great marriage.

"I, (you), take you (spouse), to be my wife/husband, to have and to hold from this day forward, for better, for worse, for richer, for poorer, in sickness and in health, to love and to cherish, till death us do part, according to God's holy law, in the presence of God I make this vow."

And if you said "I do" then do it and build good and lasting memories that you both can cherish for a lifetime.

BLAST OFF:

Let the marriage journey begin:

- Remember the obligation you committed to and be able to answer for your conduct.
- Do more than look for happiness in the marriage; bring happiness to the marriage.
- Always consider how your decisions will impact the one you say you love.
- You have been given the privilege to choose, so make wise decisions.

CHAPTER 6

FOUNDATIONS - LOVE

All humans, male and female, are created in God's own image. Because God is love; than housed within the nature of every individual is the ability to love. Everyone has a fundamental need for emotional love. The dictionary defines love in many ways. Love(n) - 1. Strong affection for another arising out of kinship or personal ties; 2. Attraction based on sexual desires; 3. Affection based on admiration; 4. Unselfish loyal and benevolent concern for the good of another; Love(v) - 1. To hold dear, cherish; 2. To feel a lover's passion; 3. To like or take pleasure in.

When Lisa and I first started attending marriage seminars in the early 1990's, the speakers addressed three Greek words that explained different types of love (Agape, Eros & Philia). Then, in the early 2000's another Greek word was added to our vocabulary (Storge). At the beginning of 2020, we did a love series and one of our daughter's presented and included four additional words that expanded the list to eight (Pragma, Philautia, Mania and Ludas).

Finally, the light bulb came on. We had often discussed why people disagreed so much on the actual meaning of our English word love. Contrasting views of the word love appears in songs, movies, and books. Why did people express themselves whereby the same word implied diverse significance? Why is there so much confusion? Is love real or imaginary? Does it come from your heart or deep inside your brain? Is love a choice or a biological response?

Since there are so many questions and views about love it was easy for Lisa and me to see why people (especially married couples) could not get on the same page regarding love. Many couples were reading different things out of different books. Which book or definition of love were they practicing, studying, or referring to? Most of the times they were not talking about the same thing. There can be no meetings of minds if two people are on different wavelengths and sending different signals.

The word love has been watered down so much that to some love had become just an ambiguous word or term. Yes, love is complex, and it can be confusing at times, but it can also be simple and understood if everyone took the time to understand the importance of it (whatever *it* may be).

How do you define love?

- **Agape**: Unconditional love or a God like love that is selfless in nature and exists regardless of changing circumstances.
- **Eros**: Romantic love or being in love. Lust, desiring pleasure, or sexual activity.

- ***Philia***: A friend bond or brotherly love. Friendships bonded by common values.
- ***Storge***: Family love or empathy bond. A liking through fondness or familiarity.
- ***Pragma***: Enduring love where couples choose to put equal effort into their relationship.
- ***Ludus***: Playful love that include activities that focus on having fun.
- ***Philautia***: Self-love that starts within oneself.
- ***Mania***: Obsessive love towards a partner that leads to codependency.

Love begins when you truly understand what love is. Love must take root with you knowing who you are. It then intensifies with you knowing the love of God. Simply put, when you love yourself and God according to God's plan, it makes it easier to love someone else. A spouse should not be added to the love equation until unconditional love is epitomized. And if you are already married, it is not too late to adopt and embrace Agape love.

Before we begin to define love in a marriage and discover how to have a successful relationship with your spouse, we must examine the perfect example of what love is in the scriptures.

John 3:16 (KJV):
' For God so loved the world, that He gave His only begotten Son, that whosoever believeth in Him should not perish, but have everlasting life. '

God did not only talk about love, but He was also willing to give His all to show his love.

I John 3:16 (KJV):
16. 'Hereby perceive we the love of God, because He laid down his life for us: and we ought to lay down our lives for the brethren.'

God presented us with a profound analogy. He is the groom, and the church is His bride. Each spouse must be willing to lay down their lives or put themselves aside and prove their love for their spouse, just as Jesus did.

Ephesians 5:31-32 (KJV):
31. For this cause shall a man leave his father and mother, and shall be joined unto his wife, and they two shall be one flesh.
32. This is a great mystery: but I speak concerning Christ and the church.

Most individuals have it out of order. They enter a relationship looking to be loved as the primary objective instead of going into the relationship looking to love. Wanting to be loved can never be minimized because it is a fundamental need of human nature. Every normal person wants to be loved and needs love to be normal.

But next level unconditional love has the mindset to give first. That is before they ever receive love in return or if they do not ever receive love in return. The husband's or wife's primary goal in marriage is to make sure they love their spouse unconditionally. The secondary goal is for the husband or wife to receive the love from their spouse if or when their spouse chooses to love in return.

"To love" must always come before "to be loved" prior to entering a marital relationship and while maintaining it. True love causes one to do what they do for their spouse without themselves in mind. This means to concentrate on your spouse and put their needs before your very own. And before you write this off as nonsense, just remember that God did it for His spouse.

Therefore, if you love and know God, you have the power to love like God if you decide to. Your understanding and acceptance of how things were designed to be and operate will be the difference between having a marital relationship with high efficiency, low efficiency, or no efficiency. The dilemma with next level love is no one really wants to get hurt, but getting hurt is sometimes a part of life. And next level love requires you to take a risk.

Love is a conscious choice to stay committed to one person. Commitment continues in the good times and bad. Many couples have realized that love itself will not keep individuals from being divorced. Throughout our marriage, Lisa and I have witnessed couples who deeply love each other go their separate ways because they did not know how to live with each other, even though they loved each other.

One of these couples we encountered was at one of our son's baseball games. While supporting our son in his athletic adventures, we had the opportunity to interact with players and their parents. In one situation we noticed one of the boy's parents were at every game. This couple sat together talking, laughing, playing, cheering, and eating from the same plate. If one of them went to the concession stand, they made sure they checked with each other. After the games, their son would come off the field, hug them and they would all walk to their cars together. Imagine how shocked we were when we found out later that season that they were divorced. Not during the season but before the season started. How? They seemed like the best of friends. They showed more love than some couples we knew who were still together. But they got along better apart than they did together.

Knowledge is power. Love is powerful. The knowledge of how to love is epic.

CHAPTER 7

FOUNDATIONS - COMMITMENT

When it comes to misunderstood words, commitment may rank in the top five. Many say they are committed, but only a few couples today actually show that they mean what they say if you look at the divorce rate and the number of couples living together without being married. A declaration without implementation is just an articulation of a proposition without assertion. In other words: it is just talking with no substance to back up what has been said.

The dictionary defines "commitment" as an agreement or pledge to do something. Marital commitment says I am not only just willing to share my body and a house, but I am personally committed to make a long-term agreement and pledge my love and life to the person I claim to love.

Commitment is exhibited through one's allegiance, dedication, loyalty, faithfulness, and steadfastness to keep the covenant with the individual you made a promise, pact, contract, or deal with. In marriage, it is with your spouse whom you have promised to love and care for the rest of your life. So, when the going gets rough, the committed hang tough. They are resilient and do not believe in leaving when things get difficult. They believe in staying for as long as they could and doing whatever it takes to try and make their marriage relationship work.

Commitment endures the good, the bad and the ugly. There are some unfortunate situations in a marriage where a couple may be forced to temporarily distance themselves. Abuse, whether physical or mental, may leave individuals with no other choice but to separate for their well-being, but they continue to pray and hope for change until the abuser refuses to change.

When a person is committed to their marital relationship, they constantly give their all to their marriage. They rejoice when things are going well and persevere when they are not. They learn to make peace if they are getting their way and if they do not. These individuals understand that working together to make each other better will make the marriage better. Covenant keeping commitments go beyond what other people say, what your feelings say, or what your emotions say.

There will be times when you may not feel in love, but commitment says keep living and keep trying until the love comes back. There will be times that you feel your heart is broken, but commitment bonds your relationship until your true love is mentally mended. Love may even seem imperfect, extreme, or unreasonable at times due to your humanity, but it remains a freedom to be chosen to enjoy and a commitment to be chosen to keep.

Couples must learn the art of teamwork in a partnership. If both partners stay true to one another (fidelity), care for one another (bonding), and enrich one another (sharing), it will make working with one another easier. Everything one spouse does should be in consideration of how their spouse will be benefited or affected.

If the two of you are to live together, be together, fight your enemies together, succeed together then you both must learn to be accountable to each other. It is the two of you against the world. No one or nothing should be able to interfere or separate you from your spouse.

Expectations are a central part of any marriage because it is the only relationship where two people become one by mutual consent. Many couples recognize the natural and physical aspects of marriage but do not understand that marriage is also spiritual.

God made the man and the woman. Then He gave each one the responsibility to ensure the happiness of the other. A committed woman loves God, respects her husband, defers to his decisions (authority) after discussing a path forward, stands with her husband, makes him better than he was when he was alone, and keeps the peace in their home. The husband should love God, love his wife like God loves the church, provide for his household, bring out the best in his wife, and protect his family. The woman was designed to complete the man, not take care of somebody's child. The man needs a help meet and not help meat that does not make him complete.

If you are truly made in God's image; you will know how to be committed and keep the covenant.

Psalm 89:34 (KJV): "My covenant will I not break, nor alter the thing that is gone out of my lips."

Be true to yourselves, your spouse, God, and your fellow person. Know the meaning of commitment. And if you feel that you are complete without a spouse, do them a favor and stay single.

CHAPTER 8

FOUNDATIONS - SACRIFICE

John 3:16 has long been a popular verse among Christians, fans, and fanatics. "For God so loved the world, that He gave His only begotten Son, that whosoever believeth in Him should not perish, but have everlasting life."

What is concealed in this beautiful verse of scripture is the sacrifice that was made for the relationship to be in a state of production and reach the full potential for development. The enigma that lies beneath the verse is what marriage should be about: giving. God gave and He wants each person in the marriage to give. Sacrifice is the secret to a successful marriage.

Sacrifice in a marriage may seem insignificant and only a small part for the overall success of togetherness, but without it, selfishness abounds. For two people to live together in peace and harmony it will always require some sort of sacrifice.

Sacrifice means to surrender something for the sake of something or someone else. It is an offering where someone suffers loss or give up something for an ideal, belief or end. A happy marriage is the ultimate object or aim of an endeavor.

People plant a seed and grow a plant, flower, or tree. They give up the seed for something greater. A spouse must be willing to sacrifice for the improvement of themselves, as well as the betterment of their spouse. God gave his best (Eve) to his best (Adam) with the plan for them to give each other their best.

The marriage vows that a couple pledges to execute on their wedding day are heavily inundated with commitments to sacrifice when necessary. You cannot have love without sacrifice and commitment. Jesus demonstrated the greatest example of commitment and sacrifice when he allowed Christ to be crucified. If someone does not see the rewards in sacrificing, they will not make a sacrifice. The more one chooses to give of themselves, the more visible and valuable they usually become to their spouse.

Sacrifice is not about being controlled or dominated, it is about humility and an interest to serve the one you love. There is nothing wrong with the perception of being hen or rooster pecked if you love the hen or rooster that is pecking you. Sacrifice is not even about competing with one another to see who can do more or less. It is about engaging in actions of compromise where the couple can work together to fulfill their dreams and accomplish their goals by coming to agreement by mutual concession.

Sacrifice allows an accommodation through a give and take process. It is not about you or me, it is about "us" and "we." Giving to gain. Loving the same.

CHAPTER 9

FOUNDATIONS - TRUST

When thinking about trust in a marriage it will be imperative to take a good look at each spouse's present truthfulness in addition to their personal experiences regarding relationships.

Present actions define who the person is and what their ethics are now. Past experiences give shape to why they choose how to trust. For most individuals, life experiences are the factors that help build a trustful attitude or develop a lack of trust.

Trust is necessary for maintaining a healthy marriage, but it is also a choice to allow someone access into areas of vulnerability where they can either lift one another up or tear one another down. Relationships that lack trust will be void of progress and will not flourish. One spouse can unintentionally devalue their mate due to the lack of trust from previous relationships.

Even the level of safety one feels in a marriage is based on the amount of trust in the person they are married to. The hierarchy of basic human needs focuses on love and safety when describing the whole person.

If the foundation of trust is destroyed or compromised in someone's formative years, it is usually manifested in withdrawal of trust due to insecurities. The individual's mindset of building a fence or wall to protect themselves from another's harmful tactics often leads to distrust in future relationships due to the perception of not being able to control all aspects of their present life.

People want to be happy, but uncontrollable suspension or uncertainty gives way to fear (false evidence appearing real). Happiness feeds on trust and joy feeds on happiness. Joy opens the door and encourages playfulness and passion. The lack of trust basically imprisons the spouse who does not trust and can alienate the spouse who may be trying to genuinely love their partner. Because of this bondage, some people are inhibited of receiving love.

To be free to love, one must be free to trust despite the risks. To have the liberty to trust, mental walls of distrust must be consciously torn down because every part of life revolves around some form of risk(s). One spouse must be afforded the opportunity to show their loyalty and love while building walls of support to obtain their partner's trust throughout their lifelong commitment.

True trust in a marriage occurs when each spouse is willing to put their lives in the hands of the other, value each other, feel safe around one another, and feel loved by one another.

CHAPTER 10

FOUNDATIONS - HONOR

Honor, by definition, is to regard someone with admiration and respect. To give them special recognition and live up to and fulfill the terms of the commitment that was made. Honor is the highest level of respect to receive and give to a person. With honor, the person and their position are highly esteemed instead of only recognizing and regarding their title.

When married couples honor one another they submit themselves to one another. They acknowledge each other's intrinsic values and how much those values mean to each other by deferring and putting their spouse ahead of themselves.

They give their all in the relationship because their spouse is first, foremost and above everyone and everything else. Honor is not about control, power, or authority, it is about self-control, submitting to one another and God's authority.

Life may change things at times, but there must be mental fortitude and determination within a person to persevere.

Perseverance must take place in the present for past promises that the couple made and for future fulfillments in the making.

The key is to keep building honor and avoiding words or actions that may tear it down. No one is perfect or does everything right. Couples must learn how to honor their spouse. The Bible says, "Love covers a multitude of sins (faults)" and Lenard and I say, "honor is for people who have good reputations."

Try your best to keep your business and shortcomings in the house. And not if, but when one spouse says or does the wrong thing or makes an unconscious mistake, let the other spouse help restore them in love. Never dishonor your spouse. Remember, you are not in competition with your spouse nor are they your enemy. The two of you are one. Therefore, do not do anything that may publicly embarrass yourself, your spouse, or your family.

Honor is a choice as well as a resource. Use it to your benefit and the well-being of your marriage. Make your spouse an important person and treat him/her as royalty. Adore them, appreciate them, acknowledge them, and love them like God does.

CHAPTER 11

FOUNDATIONS - INTIMACY

Intimacy is personal. Personal time, emotions, feelings, familiarity, contact, etc. Intimacy is intentional. It is a bonding by sharing oneself in a relationship. A connection of closeness. Events, actions, conversations, and involvements that causes a loving togetherness between two people.

Intimacy is psychological. An expression of giving love to build camaraderie, support, and trust in a relationship between parent-children, siblings, close friends, and married couples. Intimacy can be a meeting of minds where two people share ideals or experiences.

Most people usually associate intimacy with getting physically involved (kissing, carousing and sex). But you can have intimacy without being intimate. Intimacy can be sexual but does not have to be. But when intimacy occurs frequently it facilitates romance. It can be a walk in the park, a candlelight dinner with soft music, a conversation laying under the moonlight, holding hands, reciting poetry, a relaxing drive in the countryside, etc. Married couples need to learn how to set the mood for sex or making love with intimacy way before the actual encounter occurs.

Honest communication about the meanings and differences of sex and intimacy is vital to circumvent confusion or frustration in a marriage. People have different understandings and interest.

What intimacy means to one may not be what it means to the other. What sex means to one may not be what it means to the other. As stated, intimacy deals with personal closeness and sex deals with intercourse or the penetration of one's body part by another's body part.

Some have dug deeper in saying that there is a notable difference between having sex and making love. They infer that sex is just the gratification of physical desires without delicacy, gentleness, or consideration. But making love refers to intercourse derived from intimacy at different levels. Love can be involved in intimacy, but it is not always the case.

Before we move on let us pause and clarify the difference between sex in a marriage and wanting extra-ordinary sex. Consensual sex in a marriage is a part of the contract. It is expected that the two of you agree to sexual intercourse. What is acceptable and not acceptable should not only be communicated but respected by the associated spouse.

No one should be forced to engage in any sexual act or position they are not comfortable with. The objective of sex is the gratification of both parties. It is important to never rush an inexperienced spouse into uncomfortable experiences. It is important to stay within your spouse's comfort zone. What is pleasurable to one is not always pleasurable to all.

You must always consider your spouse's feelings and morals. Each spouse must ensure they are not compromising their spouse's beliefs. Be open to discuss your spouse's core values (non-negotiable) and acceptable values (negotiable). As time goes on, one spouse may become open to and accept new experiences. Then and only then is it acceptable to move forward, but not until. God does not give you anything (physically, spiritually, or mentally) that you cannot control.

Furthermore, if there is a mental disconnect due to cultural or other intrinsic factors, married couples must have honest conversations on possible reasons of why they hold back on intimacy. Because hinderances to intimacy are real and may not always be the same to everyone. It is essential that couples talk about it so that they can be about it.

Traumatic stress and insecure attachments in the past or any phase in a person's life can have a direct and indirect effect on their avoidance of intimacy. Many children raised in families where no parental bonds were developed usually struggle within relationships because psychologically, they are emotionally unstable themselves. They fear and sometimes prevent closeness to avoid being rejected or neglected.

Also, some adults avoid contact because they have been in close relationships or marriages that were abusive, (mentally or physically), where they felt betrayed; or if they were abandoned (desertion, divorce, or death) the individual affected can have a very hard time becoming open and vulnerable again. Some avoid not just intimacy, but relationships altogether.

Everyone must take the time to grow closer to their spouse over time. Some people's personalities and love languages allow them to feel comfortable around their spouses in a short time while with others it may take a while before they warm up to the closeness intimacy calls for.

The best way to overcome your past is to face your fears. The sooner open and honest communication about intimacy issues is dealt with, the sooner you can begin to feel safer to trust your spouse and allow them to accept you for who you are. For intimacy to reach the next level, a spouse must feel they are not only cared about but understood also.

CHAPTER 12

BEFORE YOU SAY "I DO"

When Lisa and I decided to get married, I scheduled a one-on-one conference with our pastor to officially discuss the "marriage" topic. We both were blessed throughout the early years of our young adult lives to be afforded many opportunities to receive impartation from Pastor Richard Allmon Sr. By serving as his deacon and driver, he and I had many personal conversations on what good marriages looked like as we traveled, ministered, and worked together. Although he had preached about it, taught about it, conversed about it, and had others in the ministry come in to do the same, I still needed reassurance and confirmation that Lisa and I were heading in the right direction.

Originally, I just wanted his blessings one more time. But as the week went on, I did not want to show up empty brained. So, I decided to go in with a profound question that would let him know I had given great thought to the matter. As soon as he opened the floor for discussion, I hit him with my strategic question intending to make him think long and hard. Smiling within I said, "I came to ask what the advantages and disadvantages are of getting married?"

Pastor Allmon leaned back in his chair and without hesitation said, "There are no disadvantages to getting married." Baffled by his quick response, I leaned forward with a quizzical look and asked him to explain. "So much for the intelligent question," I thought to myself.

He smiled and said, "There are only advantages and sacrifices in a marriage but there are no disadvantages. You will constantly need to look at how the relationship will benefit both of you and what each of you will have to give up while making the marriage work. If you perceive any area to be a disadvantage, then it is not in your best interest to get married."

Speechless, I listened on. "If the advantages outweigh the sacrifices, only then are you ready to proceed. If the sacrifices outweigh the advantages, it is best to wait. But again, there should be no disadvantages, and if there are any disadvantages, there should be no wedding."

What more could I say except "Wow!" So, with his advice in mind, we also give you this advice when it comes to making "MARRIAGE PLANS FOR TWO."

Before you make a commitment to get married, you must be sure you know what you stand to gain, and how entering in a binding relationship with the intended person will benefit you now, and long into the future. You will need to identify the compromises that you will have to make and what sacrifices will be necessary to make the relationship work.

If the perceived advantages outweigh the sacrifices, then you are ready for marriage counseling - not marriage just yet. Counseling will allow you to get a clearer picture of the advantages of entering marriage. It is wise to move into marriage, after you have sought counseling. You should only forgo counseling unless you know, without question, that this is your soul mate and there is nothing you do not know about him/her.

We tell couples marriage counseling is not necessary for everyone but recommended for all. Perceived advantages are good indicators for future success, but an impartial third-party observation can be a valuable commodity to the success of your marriage. Good counselors make counseling sessions personal. They focus on strategies to initiate open conversations to help you see your relationship (now and in a future setting) from several different perspectives. Good counselors stimulate real and in-depth discussions about any, and all, topics that can make or break your marriage in the future. Topics should include money, sex, in-laws, background, anger, friends, previous marriages, if any, etc.

If you are not ready to make the necessary sacrifices or if the sacrifices outweigh the advantages, then it would be in the best interest of both parties to postpone wedding plans until both parties have matured and are willing to fully commit to one another. Keep in mind that the emphasis will always be the disadvantages and the individual's willingness to be honest with themselves and the person they are choosing to marry. Disadvantages should be worked out before the relationship gets serious. Marriage should not be a consideration until the questionable items are addressed and resolved.

Plenty of people have chosen to be blind to the warning signs and red flags only for their eyes to come open in marriage after a disappointing or hurtful event has occurred. Most people say that "Love is Blind," but the truth is that "Marriage is a Real Eye Opener"!

Always be real and keep it real.

CHAPTER 13

WEDDING VERSUS MARRIAGE

If two people are planning on being married to each other for the rest of their lives, it is imperative that they remain "Willing, Able and Ready" to contend for the unity and sanctity of their marriage. Couples must plan to succeed in marriage.

The dictionary defines "plan" as a method for achieving an end; or to have a specified intention or design in mind to achieve an objective. The dictionary also defines "method" as a procedure or process for attaining an object; a way, technique, or process of doing something.

Therefore, Marriage Planning For Two (MP42) is a process to achieve a desired objective that is designed by God for two people to become one, and successfully build a sustainable relationship to stay together forever.

One iconic quote from our pastor's state district superintendent was "The Main Thing is to Keep The Main Thing The Main Thing." Although he was referencing one's relationship to God, the saying is also applicable to the union of marriage.

On your wedding day when you make the commitment before God and your guests, and say the two words "I Do," at that point the main thing is to keep your spouse as the main thing. You should take every precaution not to major in the minors. The primary focus of your attention should automatically become on the main thing, staying happy together while addressing the minor things amicably. The decision is up to the two of you to not allow the small foxes (situations) to destroy the vine (progress).

Together, you and your spouse must maintain a clear focus of what you desire your relationship to look like. You should set aside time to continually write the vision for your marriage on paper or in your hearts so that it is plain. This is where the effort comes in. You will need work to keep that freshly renewed vision before your eyes so that you can stay committed to each other for a lifetime.

Everyone is anxious when planning their wedding. There are so many things to plan; the ceremony, who will perform the ceremony, who will be the Maid of Honor and Best Man. What will you serve your guests at the reception? To video the event or not. All the planning and excitement leading up to the marriage can cause you to forget what is most significant. The marriage commitment that you make during that ceremony is the most important pledge of your lives together.

Your commitment to one another should always remain in the forefront of your minds and should always outweigh the excitement of the wedding day. If you must choose to be proficient in one versus the other; choose to be a professional in Marriage Planning and an amateur in Wedding Planning. The wedding ceremony can be beautiful, exquisite, entertaining, expensive, and flawless but all of that does not ensure a happy marriage.

Therefore, do not invest more time and money in your wedding plans than you do in planning the marriage with your spouse. If you invest carefully and correctly, you will generate an inseparable love that increases in value over time. A real marriage planner can help you work out the details of your goals and help you to design a strategy to approach marriage with the intentions of achieving a lifelong relationship. This marriage planner course emphasizes operating intentionally with a set purpose in all stages of your lives together.

One minor that can become a major issue is finances if both partners are not on the same page when it comes to budgeting, spending, and making large purchases together. Statistics show that finances, not sex, is the main cause of contention in relationships, before and after the wedding.

Financial transparency is crucial to avoiding unnecessary conflicts and going down the path of needless financial strain. You should discuss money usage with your partner openly, early, and often. Let them know your money values and priorities. Communicate and learn spending habits while taking notes of your partners financial strengths and shortcomings. The most important thing a couple can agree upon financially is to live within their means.

Some couples will have more money to spend than others, so you should not compare your family's financial means to others. However, all couples must realize that it is dedication to each other, not dollars, that ensure a long-term successful marriage. Life may not be fair, but do not let it get you down or discourage you. It is up to you to ensure your end is better than your beginning, no matter where you start out.

Lenard and I met in college in 1986. We eventually became best friends and got married two weeks after he graduated in 1989. We took the time to openly discuss our financial position. We knew that our love for one another and spending the rest of our lives committed to one another, was more important than waiting until if or when we could save up enough for what most consider a "Big Wedding." Therefore, we set a budget for our ceremony. Keep in mind that we got married two weeks after he graduated from college, so that did not allow us a lot of time to save up a lot of money.

Our budget for the entire wedding was $1,000. Stop laughing! I am pretty sure that everyone is thinking, "that is not enough money for a wedding." You must understand, if we or our parents had more to spend, we would have. After four years of college tuition and with my upcoming graduation the following year, $1,000 is all we could afford. Our pastor was a stickler for not spending more than you had. His advice to us was "to make sure you had a place to stay and money to pay your bills when the ceremony was over."

Through the favor and grace of God, we were able to stay within reach of our budget and have a nice wedding due to the collaborative generosity and love from the members at the church we attended. Everything came together perfectly. Our pastor counseled us out of true love, the pastor of the church I previously attended in New Orleans, (our home town and the city we wanted to get married in), allowed us to use their sanctuary, the caterer only charged for the food, a young lady who attended our home church offered me the use of her wedding dress, my brother-in-law contributed his rental car, another minister used his brand-new car to chauffeur us to the reception, and my aunt allowed us to have the reception at her house.

I asked for a three-day honeymoon on the beach. Lenard gave me just that by taking me ninety miles away to the beach in Biloxi, Mississippi. And today, over thirty years later we are still happily married, because we chose to invest more in the Marriage Plans than the wedding plans. Lenard did promise me on our honeymoon that if we stayed married to see our twentieth fifth anniversary (Silver), he would take me to renew our vows and have my dream honeymoon on the beach in Hawaii (what I really wanted for our first honeymoon).

The day after our twentieth-fourth anniversary I reminded him of his promise. Our financial marriage planning for two we agreed upon at the beginning of our matrimony prepared us to have enough money saved up to do so. My original honeymoon request was delayed but not denied. But more than the honeymoon request to Hawaii, or anything else, I was always more interested in being with him and sharing our lives together, than I was on focusing my attention on what we had or did not have.

Financial transparency is crucial to avoiding unnecessary conflicts and going down the path of needless financial strain.

CHAPTER 14

WORKING TOGETHER

It really seems redundant to emphasize the importance of planning a marriage for only two people (husband and wife). But, because the twenty-first century has gotten off track in many areas of what was considered normal thinking at one time, couples are trying to reimagine what God has already declared. They are struggling to incorporate other individuals into the institution that God has already specifically ordained, "whereby two shall become one."

When two people get married, their lives together will include other people (parents, siblings, friends, in-laws, children, etc.). Blended families require additional thought and consideration, but the core of marriage remains with the relationship between the one man and the one woman who pledged to commit their lives to each other and become one flesh by the marriage vows they took. Your spouse should always be number "1" and everyone else fills in the number "2", and any other remaining spots behind him or her.

When two individuals begin thinking about uniting in marriage and becoming one, it is time for them to start making "MARRIAGE PLANS FOR TWO" and only two. Again, others are important, but only through the marriage bond can two can become one. Your spouse must come before your parents, siblings, children, friends, job, aspirations, and wealth if you are committed to making "MARRIAGE PLANS FOR TWO."

Marriage plans must include an unwavering commitment to stay united in working together to overcome every hindrance (known and unknown) that will come to impede your growth or attempt to break up your marriage.

Outside influences may matter sometimes, but they should never affect or influence the decisions you and your spouse make together. Everyone that is connected to you should respect you and your spouse. Once the two of you become one, everyone in your inner circle should respect and take into consideration your spouse's feelings, even if they do not agree with your choice.

The wife should ensure that her husband is always treated with respect and the husband must do likewise. There should be no exceptions! If disrespect is not addressed, it will bring division to the vision you have for your relationship. The two of you should set and commit to boundaries that no one is allowed to cross. If those boundaries are pushed or crossed, the two of you should directly address that person(s).

Marriage was the first institution that God ordained, and the devil has a personal agenda to erode its foundation to destroy God's plans for a husband and wife to stay together and fulfill His purpose in and with their lives. Look back on how he tricked Adam and Eve in the garden. It is up to the two of you to honor and protect the foundation of your marriage.

When Lisa and I got married in June of 1989, we immediately began to look for marriage seminars to attend. We started in our home state at a district event which was held at a nice hotel in Alexandria, Louisiana. We had a blast and a wonderful experience.

The event was fun and entertaining. It included games tailored around marriage and featured daily events. The speaker was phenomenal. He combined Bible verses with his own real-life experiences. We quickly became more in love with each other and with attending marriage seminars.

We begin to travel both in and out of our home state to gain additional information about the intricacies of marriage. The seminars turned into encounters beyond our imagination. We soaked up all the information like dehydrated sponges. The more information we took in, the more love, respect, kindness, and compassion we were able to put out to one another.

After seeing the benefits of marriage seminars and retreats, we decided it was time to share our experiences and get more couples in our local church involved. Eventually our church began to coordinate its own events that were centered around building healthy marriages. As the interest grew, God increased our vision to expand the events to reach more couples. We organized multiday marriage events where couples could get away from day-to-day life, spend some quality time alone, and get educated on ways to enhance their marriage and rekindle their romance. As we traveled across the country, we invited special guests from around the United States to present ideas, experiences, and most importantly, the Word of God.

Our marriage conferences also taught couples ways to overcome the challenges they would face over time as life, people, and circumstances try to divide the relationship they mutually promised to build in their marriage. What we learned by attending various seminars, studying the Word of God, and praying for God inspired answers to provide wisdom to assist couples achieve God's will in their marriage is what we hope to contribute to you and your spouse throughout this book. We want to provide you with the tools to enhance your marriage experience and the marital bliss you both envisioned when you said I do on your wedding day.

For every Christian, the three most important decisions they will make in their lives are:

1. Getting Saved
2. Staying Saved
3. Getting Married.

Getting saved is essentially getting married to God. Staying saved is fundamentally continuing to love God and staying married to Him. Getting married is the decision to share your life, body, emotions, dreams, etc. with another individual who vows to share those same things with you also.

WORKING TOGETHER

Getting married to someone can be the best or worst decision a person can make in their life. Therefore, it should be done with Caution, Consultation, Consideration, and Collaboration. If the couple is not diligent and vigilant about their relationship, the attraction can become their distraction; their hope can become their fear, and their dream can become their nightmare.

Marriage has different impacts and outcomes for each couple. Some spouses look forward to the happiness and ecstasy of simply being together, while other spouses may eventually look for ways to escape so they can be apart from one another. They escape by putting on masks such as extended hobbies, overtime at work, volunteering for church or social functions, etc. You should never allow the joy that you looked forward to in marriage to turn into your sorrow. You should focus on marrying the right companion. Do not marry a prayer blocker, instead marry a prayer partner. Learn how to have a good relationship with one another, so that you can keep your marriage moving forward.

Always hold on to each other even if it means letting everything and/or everyone else go. If you stay true to your vows of "For Better or Worse" then "MARRIAGE PLANS FOR TWO" will work. You have no choice but to succeed if you follow God's plans, because the making of a positive and productive marriage is a committed process.

Marriage is an awesome phenomenon.

Marriage was the first institution that God ordained, and the devil has a personal agenda to erode its foundation...

CHAPTER 15

THE EQUATION

Because God ordained marriage it is in every couple's best interest that God be a major part of their marriage. If He is kept first and not relegated to a backup or secondary role, His presence in the relationship brings love, peace, unity, and strength.

An upward focused love for God, more than anything else, creates a flourishing inner love for yourself which allows you to express a sincere outward love for your spouse. You should always seek first the Kingdom of God so that you can love God with all your heart; all the days of your life; and love your neighbor as you love yourself. In a marriage, your spouse is your closest neighbor. You did not choose to live down the street, or around the corner, or next door to them, you chose to live in the same house with them.

The husband and wife should love each other. Both should keep God in the center of their marriage and honor him as the head of their relationship. Each must challenge themselves to love Him unconditionally, know Him intimately, trust Him with all their heart

MARRIAGE PLANS FOR TWO

and lean not to their own understanding. And if they acknowledge him in all their ways, he can direct the steps of their marriage journey.

You see, there is more assurance in the advice of an advisor when you are acquainted with them. There is more confidence in the plans of a planner if you are familiar with their previous works. One is good. Two is better. But three is best.

Ecclesiastes 4:9-12 (KJV) validates God's intention of man not being alone (Genesis 2:18). Most importantly, He highlights the reason to keep Him as an essential part of your marriage.

9. Two are better than one; because they have a good reward for their labour.

10. For if they fall, the one will lift up his fellow: but woe to him that is alone when he falleth; for he hath not another to help him up.

11. Again, if two lie together, then they have heat: but how can one be warm alone?

12. And if one prevail against him, two shall withstand him; and a threefold cord is not quickly broken.

The cross is supported vertically and extended horizontally. If the two did not intersect and have a meeting point, then it would not be a cross. Individually they are just two beams or boards. But, fastened together and lifted where the vertical beam (Jesus) can hold the horizontal beam (husband/wife)

much higher than the surface, they become a structure that symbolizes hope.

Hope is symbolized when the enemy tries to mar what God is trying to age. The devil wants to ruin or dimmish the perfection or wholeness of your marriage, but Jesus wants to keep it intact.

John 10:10 (KJV) defines the enemy's and God's intentions for your marriage, your life, and your family.
10. The thief cometh not, but for to steal, and to kill, and to destroy: I am come that they might have life, and that they might have it more abundantly.

A marriage sails along smoothly, and the couple has fun sailing and enjoying each other until their vessels meet the storms of life. Marital storms or trials and tribulations can spoil a cheerful sunny day. These trials can cause discontinuity in a loving bond due to the concern, anguish, and suffering that the couple must endure. But prayer can change things. Maintaining a strong faith in Jesus can keep the marriage relation*ship* afloat. A prepared couple has no anxiety or trepidation of the raging waves, howling winds and tumultuous commotion. Instead, they are poised, confident, and steadfast knowing that if their faith is in God, they will overcome any obstacle that they may face. If their faith in God remains firm and their hope continues to be strong, they know that God can still the storms or redirect their marriage around the storms. With God as their captain, the couple is equipped and prepared to make it through all of life's challenges.

Instructions on how to navigate through storms, and apply marriage safety training, is found in the Word of God. Navigational and safety trainings are part of the package when you sign up for the marriage journey. Your knowledge and preparation in what should be done in a crisis will be the difference between having a good chance of survival or being vulnerable to the dangerous elements. A good marriage does not happen by accident. You must anchor your marriage in the Word of God and expect the unexpected to prevent the preventable.

If two individuals actively love God with all their heart, mind, soul, and strength, then they will keep his commandments. By doing so, they will keep their marriage whole as it flourishes.

God designed marriage as a partnership and not a sole proprietorship or a corporation with a board of directors. The dictionary defines "partnership" as a relationship resembling a legal partnership and usually involving close cooperation between two parties having specified and joint rights and responsibilities.

Both individuals must come ready to make it a successful business with benefits. Both will have to give 100% and their best effort for their business to be effective. Each should have a clear knowledge of who handles what responsibilities within the marriage. This should be a result of ongoing communication between the couple. Pride should be pushed aside and comparing themselves to how somebody else does it should not be a factor.

In a good business partnership, the individual with the most knowledge and ability to produce a desired and prudent outcome is the one chosen to manage those responsibilities or specialty. In

God's plan for marriage, He envisioned a team concept instead of two independent individuals working separately. In fact, before mankind had natural parents, God provided a marital perspective that provided order for future couples.

Genesis 2:24 (KJV):
24. Therefore shall a man leave his father and his mother and shall cleave unto his wife: and they shall be one flesh.

To become one flesh there must be some leaving, cleaving, and believing. The man should leave where he came from and cleave to who he vowed to be with. He should leave his daddy's or mama's house and become his own man with his wife in their own house. The only woman a man should leave to be with his wife is his mother. His wife must come second only to God.

Biblical truth tells us that God ordained the matrimonial union. Marriage is to be between one man and one woman for a lifetime. One man joined to one woman equals one flesh. God's example of biblical marriage can be equated as:

<u>Biblical Marriage</u>
1 man X 1 woman = 1 flesh.

<u>Worldly Marriage</u>
1 man + 1 woman = 2 individuals.

Throughout the Bible, we can clearly see that God is in the multiplying business. He himself created the blueprint for marriage, ordained the first marriage, and made Adam to be with Eve. He did not include Evonne and/or Evette. He made Eve for

Adam and did not include Steve and/or Stuart. God was so serious about making a suitable helper that He made Eve using the part of Adam's body that is closest to his heart - his rib.

He did not make Adam and Steve or Evonne and Eve. He created male and female, man and woman, husband, and wife. Anything outside of God's original intent and equation of only two people (of the opposite sex) for marriage equals confusion.

Christians must watch and pray before and after the wedding. Pray to God and watch and see what type of relationship your fiancé/ fiancée or spouse has with God. Their relationship with God will be a good litmus test on how their relationship will be with you. In most cases, if a man cannot love and honor God, he may have problems loving and honoring his wife. Likewise, if a woman cannot submit to and obey God then she may have difficulties submitting to and obeying her husband. (I Peter 3:1-7; Ephesians 5:22-33; Colossians 3:18-19)

When a husband loves and honors his wife, he is showing his affection for her. When a wife submits to and obeys her husband, she is showing respect for him. As mentioned earlier, we are not speaking of submission as a subservient role but acknowledging that due to God's biblical order in marriage, the wife, after discussing any matter that may arise, may at times have to defer to her husband's final decision if it is in the Lord (not outside the written Word of God).

When opinions collide, a couple must be willing to hear one another's thoughts, see one another's views and feel one another's convictions to settle on a common resolution, keep harmony, and have a good relationship with each other. Even if both parties cannot come to terms, they must learn to respectfully agree to disagree to enjoy a healthy partnership. At the end of the day, Lisa and I must give this disclaimer: "We did not make the rules of the game; we simply communicate and play by the rules given."

-Marriage factors from a biblical worldview:
HUSBAND = WIFE
HUSBAND's Role = LOVE + HONOR
WIFE's Role = SUBMIT + RESPECT (OBEY)

Therefore:
LOVE + HONOR = SUBMIT + RESPECT (OBEY)

This is a balanced equation that must be maintained to keep unity and harmony in the marriage. If either side is lacking or not in equilibrium, then one spouse can balance the equation by increasing the output on their side of the equation. If the husband is not showing enough affection to his wife, she can balance his lack of affection with more respect, consideration, and attention until his affection increases. Likewise, if the wife is not showing enough respect to her husband, he can balance her lack of respect with more love, assurance, and tenderness until her respect increases.

The married man should be concerned about how to please and have a good relationship with his wife and the married woman should be concerned about how to please and have a good relationship with her husband (I Corinthians 7:33-34).

Husbands, your wives should be shown affection and a whole lot of it. God wired women to want emotional affection, psychological affection, physical affection, and financial affection. This allows her to feel secure in her marriage, helping her to yield to her husband's headship. It does not matter if she makes more money or is more spiritual, she wants to know she is taken care of and protected. A woman can learn to make it on her own, but that is why she married you and calls you husband.

Wives, your husbands need to feel important and be treated like he is important to you. He wants to be respected in every way. You can show your respect in the way and tone that you talk to him, the way that you respond to his requests and decisions, and especially how you treat him around others. He does not want to be Lord of your life; he just wants to be treated like the lord in your life. Remember to always give him a little praise and pump up his self-esteem here and there. Avoid the pattern of continuously deflating his ego and constantly criticizing him and his efforts.

Wives, always lift your husbands up (compliment). Husbands, in no way put your wives down (never insult). Pay attention to the words shared in the book of Song of Solomon if you do not believe in giving compliments or cannot refrain from insults. God not only receives praise, but He also advises couples to praise each other.

Wife to her husband (Song of Solomon 5:11-16 (KJV):

11. His head is as the most fine gold, his locks are bushy, and black as a raven.

12. His eyes are as the eyes of doves by the rivers of waters, washed with milk, and fitly set.

13. His cheeks are as a bed of spices, as sweet flowers: his lips like lilies, dropping sweet smelling myrrh.

14. His hands are as gold rings set with the beryl: his belly is as bright ivory overlaid with sapphires.

15. His legs are as pillars of marble, set upon sockets of fine gold: his countenance is as Lebanon, excellent as the cedars.

16. His mouth is most sweet: yea, he is altogether lovely. This is my beloved, and this is my friend, O daughters of Jerusalem.

Husband to his wife (Song of Solomon 7:1-9 (KJV):

1. How beautiful are thy feet with shoes, O prince's daughter! the joints of thy thighs are like jewels, the work of the hands of a cunning workman.
2. Thy navel is like a round goblet, which wanteth not liquor: thy belly is like an heap of wheat set about with lilies.
3. Thy two breasts are like two young roes that are twins.
4. Thy neck is as a tower of ivory; thine eyes like the fishpools in Heshbon, by the gate of Bath-rabbim: thy nose is as the tower of Lebanon which looketh toward Damascus.
5. Thine head upon thee is like Carmel, and the hair of thine head like purple; the king is held in the galleries.
6. How fair and how pleasant art thou, O love, for delights!
7. This thy stature is like to a palm tree, and thy breasts to clusters of grapes.
8. I said, I will go up to the palm tree, I will take hold of the boughs thereof: now also thy breasts shall be as clusters of the vine, and the smell of thy nose like apples;
9. And the roof of thy mouth like the best wine for my beloved, that goeth down sweetly, causing the lips of those that are asleep to speak.

A many of couples, who loved each other, have gone their separate ways because they felt like they were not treated right. The wife says she was overlooked, under-valued, and under-appreciated. The husband says he heard everything he did wrong and not enough of what he did right.

You cannot construct what you consume. Neither can you build a relationship that you continually destroy. Some things cannot be undone, some words cannot be taken back once said, so be very careful how you react when you get angry, frustrated, or disappointed. It is true, "actions speak louder than words." Words have their voice also and can express both the good, as well as the bad in a marriage. A soft answer turns away wrath and constant criticism and complaining separates the best of friends, and that includes husbands and wives. As Christians you must always stay cognizant of who you represent.

Philippians 2:13-15 (KJV):

13. For it is God which worketh in you both to will and to do of his good pleasure.
14. Do all things without murmurings and disputings:
15. That ye may be blameless and harmless, the sons of God, without rebuke, in the midst of a crooked and perverse nation, among whom ye shine as lights in the world.

The more couples yield to God, the more they will listen to and respect each other. Your spouse's opinions may not make sense, but they should matter.

CHAPTER 16

SIMILAR BUT DIFFERENT

The man and the woman were created by God differently and distinctly, but also similar in many ways. God formed man from the dust of the ground and breathed life into His creation and he became a living soul.

But He formed the woman, a living soul also, from the rib of the man and then brought His new creation unto His original creation to become one, separated but united; two people, personalities, and powers but one unit and team.

The man and woman have spirits, souls, and bodies. Both have yearnings to be pleased physically, visually, sexually, mentally, and spiritually. They have similar skeletal frames and bodily functions. However, there are some visual and non-visual body parts and usefulness that make them uniquely male and female.

Researchers and psychologists have fun trying to list the biological, physiological, and cognitive similarities and differences. They look to compare genetics, body mass, emotional, behavioral, and developmental distinctions. At the end of the day there are differences that must be noted and should be understood. Especially when marriage is involved.

But the fact that God was the author and creator behind it all lets us know that there was a purpose for the resemblances and diversities. He did not create one to be better than the other. He created them to complement one another. In fact, the differences are the attractions and challenges that make the interactions between husbands and wives more interesting. Everyone must remember that it was God who declared, "It is not good that the man should be alone; I will make him a help meet for him." (Genesis 2:18 (KJV):

God's intention was to make a being that would balance and complete the man he originally created. If happily married couples were asked, they would agree that God did a very good job with the physical differences. A lot of them are still undecided or puzzled by the psychological differences that exists.

Whether you agree or disagree, God had an objective in every part of creation. Mankind and their differing cultures have created stereotypes that attempt to direct their males and females in the perceptions of preset values, principles, and beliefs. Boys are usually expected to be rough, and girls are typically expected to be gentle. Men are looked upon as weak if they cry and women are looked upon as defiant if they are aggressive. However, there comes a time when real men cry and when real women must take the lead.

The idea that some roles are interchangeable is hard to comprehend for some, especially in a marriage. We must remember that the woman was designed to complete her husband, not compete with or against him. No one thought David was less of a man, less known the king, when he wept in the loss of his child. The Proverbs 31 husband flourished with a strong woman because he knew his purpose and was not intimidated by hers.

If you read it carefully, he praised her because she was adding to his life and helping him fulfill his purpose. She came equipped to help with virtue, wisdom, hard work, goals, intellect, ideas, etc. and her self-value was shown in everything she did. She did not have to get frustrated because her husband had a vision. His vision only fueled her vision and further strengthened her confidence and self-esteem.

Her husband was known in the gates because the men of the city saw a Godly couple. They witnessed a man who loved his wife and a wife that respected her husband. We do not know who was in charge behind closed doors, which one handled the finances they both made, or who made most of the decisions in their home and business lives? Did it really matter? Their consistencies may have been other couples' disparities. The example is proof that if they honored their God given roles the variances did not matter.

Is it true that men process words with their logic and women process words with their feelings? If so, it may explain why marriages are a little difficult for some husbands and wives to appreciate. They have a desire to "want to" be there for each other, they just do not understand each other as much as they initially thought.

Women must be familiar with how their husbands think and adjust until a balance is found. And the men, likewise, must understand how their wives process their feelings and adjust until balance is found. What Lenard and I came to realize is that husbands and wives speak words with good intentions, most of the time, but the words are sometimes received by their partner as negative or confrontational because they process their spouse's words through their own mind and how they think instead of through their spouse's mind and their way of thinking.

A good listener learns to process information from the sender's point of view in addition to their own point of view. This allows them to see things from both perspectives. One married person may not particularly agree with their spouse, but they should have studied their partner long enough to know what past factors are influencing their present sensitivities. They should also learn to phrase their question or response in a nonconfrontational way to reach the best possible outcome to maintain harmony in their marriage.

Women, for the most part, are sharers and nurturers. They like to talk about their thoughts, feelings, and experiences. They enjoy relationships where they can openly contribute and feel valued for their input. But sometimes, unknowing to them, women, especially wives, have a way of overly conveying information when they become emotionally involved. When they go into "advice mode" they may unconsciously reiterate the same deficiencies repeatedly. What the wife intends to be "assistive communication" is received as nagging by her husband.

Because most men are results oriented, most do not immediately take other people's feelings into consideration and their actions or tones makes their wives feel rejected. Unconsciously, the husband's primary focus can shift from seeking a solution to finding a way to redirect or end the conversation. The negative words or responses from husbands can severely affect their wives because women usually process words with their feelings. If her feelings are wounded, she looks at the situation as unfriendly or mean. The more unfriendly encounters wives have with their husbands, the less they want to share themselves because constant use of negative words causes some wives to withhold positive emotions.

Because wives often feel torn down by the constant verbal abuse or stern confrontations from their husbands, they become vulnerable to optimistic admiration from others. Constant, unfriendly encounters at home can have wives dreading going home to their husbands. Constant, friendly encounters at work or other settings leave wives looking forward to going to those places rather than going home to the actual or perceived abuse.

Husbands must find ways to make their wives feel special, even when they must keep it real with them. The devil has a way of influencing other men to be friendly to wounded wives by telling them what they want to hear and by making them feel wanted.

Husbands do not always master addressing what their wives are asking for either. A lot of husbands think their wives are always looking for solutions to their issues or verbalized concerns when truthfully their wives just want to be heard. Husbands and wives that work must practice transitioning from the "go mode" to the "slow mode" when they get home from work. After allowing each other a time to unwind and settle, the spouses should prioritize spending time with each other.

The husband must be sensitive and leave space in his evening schedule to listen to his wife. The wife must be wise and incorporate a little praise for her husband in her conversations to keep his attention and interest.

In fact, compliments are always healthy for the marriage. The wife should make it a point to constantly compliment her husband to communicate her affections. As the wife, you may have the right motive, but another woman may not. Wives commend your husbands. If you are praising your husband regularly, it should be nothing new or extra to your husband to hear another woman praise or compliment him. The Bible says that "The full soul loatheth an honeycomb; But to the hungry soul every bitter thing is sweet" Proverbs 27:7 (KJV

Now, because most husbands process words with their logic, the wife must be cognizant of what her communications, words, and actions may be conveying to her husband through his thought process.

Laughably, most men have been classically conditioned; especially when it is sex related. For example, if the wife tells her husband she has a headache when she comes to bed, instead of getting a Tylenol or Aspirin, he turns over and assumes she is saying no sex tonight. If she decides to wear something comfortable, but sexy, to bed after taking her bath, he automatically assumes she either wants or is offering sex tonight.

Most men think about sex a lot, so it is an area of marriage that must be addressed often. Someone once said, "A lot of young women think their husband is possessed because they want sex all the time and a lot of middle-aged women wished their husbands were possessed sometimes." Although somethings differ from couple to couple, some things are elementary. Truer affection, regard, and friendliness may lead to more sex in the marriage.

But if the truth be told, a lot of men just lack understanding when it comes to the availability of sex. This is because they do not experience the type of stress and monthly bodily changes that women do (i.e. - hormonal imbalances, menstrual cramps, postpartum depression, etc.). Women change seasons often, whereas the apparent needs of men do not.

When you align the needs of the husband with the right season of his wife you will have harmony and experience a beautiful melody. But when a couple is out of alignment and out of season there is chaos.

The husband must learn to recognize and be sensitive to his "wife's seasons." He must watchfully discern her times and episodes because wife seasons do not operate in sequence like nature (Winter, Spring, Summer, and Autumn). A wife's seasons can change as fast as the weather in south Louisiana. A husband must be ready to adjust at any time.

When she is in her Winter season, leave her alone. She can be cold and freeze your plans, thoughts, and emotions in their tracks.

When she is in her Autumn season, conditions are getting better, but you do not know if there will be sunshine, rain, frost, or snow, day by day. When she is in her Spring season, you will notice her warming up to you (her husband) as she starts to bloom, and everything comes back to life. When she is in her Summer season, the temperature is hot, and the coast is clear. She will be ready to be cooled off so the husband must come prepared to shower her.

Husbands have two main seasons: Summer and Autumn. You may get a day or two of Spring and Winter, but because their minds are usually tropical, it does not take much to make it Summertime again.

How can two people be so much alike and be so different at the same time? We cannot say, but marriage has the answer. You and your spouse should have a few "Garden of Eden" days and be naked and not ashamed a few times a year.

CHAPTER 17

OPPOSITES ATTRACT

When I was a teenager, I would always hear people say, "Opposites attract each other in relationships." Now that I am older, I really understand what they were saying.

Lisa and I are different in so many ways. Our personalities are opposites in all the personality assessments we took part in. The D.I.S.C. assessment categorized me in the Dominance (D) group and Lisa in the Steadiness (S) group. In the Humourism assessment I am labeled Fire (Choleric), and she is labeled Water (Phlegmatic). In the Christian assessment I am characterized as a Lion (Strong and Assertive), and she is categorized as a Golden Retriever (Compassionate and Loyal). But our differences complement our relationship instead of taking from it. Most of my strengths are her shortcomings and her strengths are my shortcomings. We bring harmony to our marriage by not just acknowledging the differences, but also by allowing each other to freely operate in one another's inherent assets. If Lisa's strong attributes are more effective in an area to facilitate accomplishing our united goal, then

I support her and vice-versa. Two can only walk together if there is agreement (Amos 3:3).

One spouse may only see a color (i.e., green) while the other spouse sees shades of the same color (olive, lime, hunter, forest, or aqua green). One spouse sees the details of the mission while the other spouse only sees the mission. Is that a problem? We do not think so. Can it be a problem? Yes, it can, but only if the couple allows it to manifest into one. The key is to take notice of what the two of you agree on: Green. Then, appreciate the distinctive originality God created in each of you.

The underlying goal is to learn to work together as a TEAM to reach the ultimate goals you both established. If you can operate as one with humility and not pride, everybody benefits. Your marriage will benefit, your children will benefit, your family will benefit, and the Kingdom of God will benefit. Marriage must be a give and take relationship that is carried out by each person. There must be love and mutual respect.

Men and women are wired differently and may not think alike all the time. But no married couple should lose sight of the united long-term objectives by only focusing on short-term individual problems. Your pain, your hurts, your wants, and your needs are important and will need to be addressed without losing focus of the reason you married one another.

Just because you see situations or challenges differently does not indicate that there is a problem or the ruining of your marriage. This simply provides more ways to draw you closer to one another to approach situations, solve problems, answer questions as you navigate through this journey called life. Two heads are better than one. There should be a joint effort to promote the growth and continual development of each other's talents and ambitions to ensure the successful building of "US."

I Peter 3:10-11 provides five suggestions that every married couple can implement to keep their relationship real.

I Peter 3:10-11 (KJV):
1. For he that will love life, and see good days, let him refrain his tongue from evil, and his lips that they speak no guile:
2. Let him eschew evil, and do good; let him seek peace, and ensue it.

If your goal in marriage is to love life and see good days, then the Bible admonishes you to:

a. Keep your tongue from evil
b. Keep your lips from speaking guile
c. Eschew evil
d. Do good
e. Seek and pursue peace

a. You can never take back words so be careful what you tell someone about the person you say you love. Your spouse is not perfect, but they are real. They are not a finished product, and like you, may be in a "work in progress" state of their life when questionable decisions are made. If you make reactive statements that slander, defame, or diminish their character, you cannot go back and retract your words. It is like opening a feathered pillow and releasing the feathers in a field. Even if you decide to restore your pillow it will be impossible to get all the original feathers back. Besides that, you may look misleading if you decide to stay or take them back. So, speak no evil.

b. It is impossible to be totally honest with the person you say you love if deceit is anywhere in the picture. Guile is fraudulent dishonesty and has no place in a marriage. When someone is causing someone else to accept something to be true or valid and their words are not meaningful or they are not being real or one hundred with the other person, it is a lie. Never lie to the ones you love. Speak no guile.

c. It is impossible for you to please God or your spouse if you love what God hates and hates what God loves. Despite what is acceptable to the world, social media, or people you call friends, right is still right and wrong is still wrong as it pertains to God's word. Do not let the devil fool you; God hates evil and loves righteousness. The fear or respect of God is the beginning of knowledge and understanding. Just like God loves the sinner and not the sin, you must love your spouse despite some of their shortcomings. The husband and the wife should keep themselves from any morally wrong conduct despite how they feel, what their spouse has done, or how much they are hurt and disappointed. Eschew evil.

d. You cannot really say you truly love someone until they mean just as much to you as yourself. When a person reaches the level of maturity where they do unto others as they would have someone else do unto them, they are in a good place. Then they are free to always do the right thing.

To be kind, benevolent, and virtuous is a choice in a marriage. You must have the passion to make your spouse happy regardless of what they are doing or are not doing to make you happy. Do good.

e. You cannot fight the "good fight" and be victorious spiritually if you are fighting the wrong fights naturally. Love and fighting do not go together. They are enemies unless you are fighting to keep your marriage together. You can love what you are fighting for but should not be fighting who you love. Love and peace do go together, and they are harmonious. Jesus said, "My peace I give to you" because he knew that you would need it. In times like these your mind needs to be free from oppressive thoughts or emotions. Most of all, both husbands and wives must learn when to speak and when it would be best to keep silent for the overall good of their marital relationship. Seek peace.

Marriage is not a sprint; it is a lifelong marathon. Pace yourself and run that you may obtain, prepare for the long haul, and increase your endurance. Hold on, hope on, carry on and continue on. Be the greatest spouse your husband/wife can imagine.

There should be a joint effort to promote the growth and continual development of each other's talents and ambitions to ensure the successful building of "US."

CHAPTER 18

LIVE RESPONSIBLE

I Corinthians 7: 2 (KJV):
'Nevertheless, to avoid fornication, let every man have his own wife, and let every woman have her own husband.'

Everyone everywhere must clearly understand that God promotes sex in the proper context. He created the male and female with different body types and functions for that purpose. He created the man and the woman to be able to join themselves together physically, biologically, mentally, emotionally, socially, and spiritually as husband and wife. He then authorized them to have sex, be fruitful, and multiply.

In fact, God gave man His best when He created the woman. She is a well thought out and appealing masterpiece, the greatest machine God ever designed. She was created with all the right functions, buttons, curves, and accessories. Eve came fully loaded, fully equipped, and compatible to Adam in every way. Adam said, "Bone of my bone and flesh of my flesh" in excitement when he saw Eve. God said He did not want the man to be alone, so He did something about it. Eve, in return, received God's best when she was introduced to Adam.

Adam was provided with intelligence and an ingenious tool to work the garden of Eve. You never read anywhere of Eve complaining to God about what He equipped Adam with.

Then they gave each other the best of their best. God's expectation was, and always will be, for married couples to appreciate and enjoy each other and to always put Him and His word above the best that they have received from Him. Enjoy your spouse but keep God first and stay within the boundaries He established.

We see that God chose and ordained marriage and sex to be enjoyed between a husband and his wife. Every man is to have his own wife (singular) and every woman is to have her own husband (singular). He did not include a "sidepiece" agreement, permit test drives, hook-ups, single friends with benefit packages, and open relationship deals.

Hebrews 13:4 (KJV):"Marriage is honorable in all, and the bed undefiled:..."

God also asked everyone in Proverbs 5:3 to "Drink waters out of thine own cistern and running waters out of thine own well." Partake of the one that you have pledged yourself to.

God designed the sexes to be attracted and attractive to each other, but He also made rules if you want to play the game. So, let us go back to verse one.

I Corinthians 7:1 (KJV):
'Now concerning the things whereof ye wrote unto me: It is good for a man not to touch a woman.'

The rule says it is not good for a man to touch a woman unless he is married to her. Many assume this applies only to physical touch, but it primarily applies to mental touching. On the most part, if someone can touch a woman mentally, she will be more likely to allow them to touch her physically. If her mind could be penetrated with words or deeds whereby it touches her thoughts and feelings and she perceives that she is admired or loved, then someone has effectively touched her mentally.

To many, that mental touch provokes embedded feelings for her to want to share herself sexually. I heard a family counselor on the radio as a young adult explain how boys/men will project love (i.e., say I love you) to get sex from a girl/woman and the girl/woman in return gives sex to receive love (true or imaginary).

Our pastor taught us that because most women are affected by touch, men should watch their words and attitudes in dealing with them because females are sometimes affected or aroused by what they hear. Flirting, untimely compliments, suggestive comments, playful touching, etc., may send the wrong signals. Men must watch not only what they say to women, but how they say it also. The wrong body language or tone may be the tipping point. He also taught that most men are affected or aroused by sight, by what they see.

Therefore, he instructed the females to watch what they wear, or do not wear, so they would not intentionally or unintentionally send the wrong signals, leave no imagination to the shape of their bodies, or cause a man to lust after the flesh he sees.

Fashion designers have even tapped into the biblical principles addressing females and their apparel/garments. Men designers usually base their women and men designs on what is appealing to their lustful eyes.

But when a husband can touch his wife mentally, he can touch her physically and when a wife dresses and presents herself so her husband can be aroused at what he sees; oh, happy day for the two of them.

I Corinthians 7:3 (KJV):
'Let the husband render unto the wife due benevolence: and likewise, also the wife unto the husband.'

Husbands are obligated to surrender, deliver, yield, or give up themselves to take care of their wives' sexual needs and the wives are admonished to do likewise. They are to furnish, deliver, offer up, and sacrifice themselves for each other according to scripture. God gave each spouse a product to be productive in the relationship and therefore both should produce without excuse. Get your rest, take your Tylenol if necessary, and prepare yourself to give to, or be received by, your spouse sexually. If you must take off work or leave a little early sometimes, then so be it. Do what you must do to keep the fire burning. There may be times where you must give a piece to get some peace.

But moderation and consideration must be in order in a marriage relationship. Some individuals have higher sex drives than their spouses. This can apply to either the husband or wife. Sexual desires can also shift as you age. The spouse that was the aggressor early in the marriage may become the contender in the latter part of the marriage. The hunter may become the hunted.

To avoid confusion and ill feelings, this should be a serious and ongoing discussion where both the husband and the wife can openly discuss their sexual needs and how they will be met. Communication is always the key. You should agree on a reasonable number of days and/or times a week that suits both of you. Compromise if you must.

I Corinthians 7:4 (KJV):
'The wife hath not power of her own body, but the husband: and likewise, also the husband hath not power of his own body, but the wife.'

When you both said, "I do," you did. You became one flesh and created a partnership. Therefore, you are co-owners of everything, including each other. Your body is no longer just your own. You maintain your primary body and your spouse maintains their primary body. But when you look at the technicalities of becoming one flesh, you both have a cut of the other.

You each have a say so about your own bodies, but there is not exclusive authority once you are married. Both parties must learn how to submit themselves one to another. Then each spouse must consider their spouse before they consider themselves. Be considerate of one another and take care of your spouse's sexual needs. There will be times when the wife sacrifices to please her husband and there will be times the husband sacrifices to please his wife. Teamwork. And if there are any misunderstandings, refer to verse three.

I Corinthians 7:5 (KJV), reinforces this by stating:
'Defraud ye not one the other, except it be with consent for a time, that ye may give yourselves to fasting and prayer; and come together again, that Satan tempt you not for your incontinency.'

Technically, the only time a married couple should abstain from sex is when they have communicated and agreed to the reason(s) why.

The Bible gives specific instructions around refraining for spiritual reasons such as fasting and special praying. Naturally, you should regard your spouse and abstain for illnesses, menstruation, and occasionally for work schedules, doctor appointments or fatigue. Self-control should be the responsibility of every individual, especially a Christian.

But self-sacrifice should replace selfishness when it comes to meeting the needs and sometimes wants of your spouse. One spouse should never use their body as leverage or manipulation against their spouse. We refer to it as "reversed extortion." The dictionary defines extorting as to obtain from a person by force, intimidation, or undue legal power. The scripture never says that you cannot give it to get what you want from your spouse; it just says that you should not hold it back to get what you want.

Be prepared to continually adjust when you marry. No two people are exactly alike. They may have similarities, but like their fingerprints, they are unique. If two people are not exactly alike, that means no two relationships will be exactly alike.

Do not compare or base your relationship on another couple's relationship. The Bible advises us to not compare ourselves among ourselves. Most importantly, do not base or compare your spouse to someone you dealt with in a previous relationship. Dragging a previous relationship in a present marriage has disaster written all over its future. You vowed to love your spouse for who they are as an individual.

Marriage is not a maintenance free relationship. Marriages need plenty of continuous checking, work, re-work, improvements, and development because the dynamics and individuals do not stay the same.

Maturity brings about changes (physical, emotional, psychological, educational, sexual, etc.). Some spouses have reimagined their lives and careers and their spouses must respect and accept those changes. As you have aged and gone through life, you are not technically married to the same person you said I do to 5/10/20/40 years ago. You must continually perform in-depth, comprehensive studies and analyses of your spouse to continually make the necessary adjustments as changes occur over time.

Marriage includes fun, but it mainly consists of work. If you enjoy who you work for and the job that you do, it is no longer considered a job. It becomes a pleasure.

The inability to change over time may cause your spouse to physically check out. Usually, you can see the early warning signs if you are paying attention to your marriage. Your spouse will usually check out mentally or psychologically before they check out physically.

The key word is STUDY!!! Learn to study your spouse from the day you think about marrying them until the day death separates you. The suffix -"ology" is commonly used in the English language to denote a field of study.

Archaeology - the study of past human activity.
Biology - the study of life and the body.
Geology - the study of the earth.
Psychology - the study of mental functions and behaviors.
Theology - the study of religious faith and practices.

You must, for the good of your marriage, specialize in (*your spouse's name*)-ology. It is called Spouseology - the study of one's spouse. And it never hurts if you get a minor in Soulology - the study of the mind, conscience, will, intellect, emotions, and passions. Relationships at all levels are about discovery.

If you are a wise spouse, you will not just do it for them; you will do it for yourself also. You need to know what makes them go and how they tick from the inside out. The day you stop studying and learning your spouse is the day that your relationship will stand still. Lenard did not become a "Lisa-ologist" overnight. It has taken years of study to get to where he currently is today. Greater still, the best is yet to come.

If you are dating/courting, there is so much you can learn about your prospective spouse and so much they can learn about you. You all will have a lifetime of discovery to enjoy yourselves after you say I do. So, make sure you save some things for the marriage. God's way is the best way.

CHAPTER 19

UNCHAINED LOVE

Your eyes will never comprehend everything you see. Look beyond sight and see the vision for your marriage.

Seasons do not matter when you enjoy who you are with. So do not let a rainy day deprive you of sunshine in the future. There is a time and season for everything. Marriage is not the end; it is the beginning. Get married to stay married and say I will when you say I do.

"MARRIAGE PLANS FOR TWO" is what you must do. Men and women may not have all the right answers; but God does.

Lisa and I have met with and counseled many "broken" people over the last thirty plus years that we have been married. And by broken we mean not whole mentally or emotionally due to being violated or damaged by people in their past. They have undergone or been subject to some form of abuse and have been made weak, sorrowful, infirmed and/or disconnected.

Their minds, hearts or spirits are no longer working properly due to irregularities, pain, guilt, or sufferings. They may feel deserted, separated, lonely or confused. But they want to love and be loved. They want to be free to move on with their lives, build meaningful relationships and be happily married. The problem is their past in the present keeps limiting their future.

Our study of love in relations to relationships has brought us to the conclusion that love is designed for the present and the future. Love cannot change the past because it happened already. Love is unable to go back in time and fix what was broken.

But love can mend what is broken over time if you allow it to. To mend is to restore, repair, improve or put into good order something or someone that has been injured, damaged or broken. Love is a game changer as well as a life changer for your tomorrows. If you combine love with forgiveness, it will allow you to bury hurts from your yesterdays.

I Peter 4:8 (KJV):
And above all things have fervent charity among yourselves: for charity shall cover the multitude of sins.

I Peter 4:8 (AMP):
Above all, have fervent and unfailing love for one another, because love covers a multitude of sins [it overlooks unkindness and unselfishly seeks the best for others].

If you choose to embrace love, it will begin the healing process and cover you and your spouse's past injuries and shortcomings. If you ignore love and it leads to a broken bond, the deep wounds and broken heart will be more difficult to heal the next time.

But if you trust the process, love can transform lives and convert negative energy to positive power. That positive power will give you peace of mind in the present and future as it restores the piece or section of mind scarred in the past. God's power to heal is greater than a person's power to hurt. There is no fear in love, therefore fear has no place in a marriage that was ordained by God.

II Timothy 1:7 (KJV):
For God hath not given us the spirit of fear; but of power, and of love, and of a sound mind.

I John 4:18 (KJV):
There is no fear in love; but perfect love casteth out fear: because fear hath torment. He that feareth is not made perfect in love.

Love can mend what is broken over time if you allow it to.

CHAPTER 20

IDENTIFY WHERE YOU ARE

In all our years of working with and counseling couples, Lenard and I have come to appreciate the couples who are open minded when it comes to making their marriages better.

Like many other issues, the first step in fixing marital problems is for the couple to admit that there is a problem. The second step is deciding if they will either: live with the problem; go their separate ways and avoid the problem; or do something positive about the problem. The last step is amicably working through the problem and achieving progress until it is fixed so they can move forward together and be happy.

Lenard and I put together seven categories of marriage and definitions for each. And it does not take long to identify which category of marriage a couple is in after having a heart-to-heart conversation with them.

a. Fascinating
b. Rewarding
c. Satisfying

d. Maintaining
   e. Struggling
   f. Disappointing
   g. Distressing

We converse with couples and ask questions to encourage dialogue between the husband and wife to evaluate how they communicate, deal with disagreements or conflicts, complement each other, and respect each other and their words. We then do relationship triage and sort the married couples into one of the seven categories to prioritize our path forward and determine what resources will be needed to give the proper advice.

With hard work and selflessness, any good marriage can be maintained, and any broken marriage can be fixed. But, if anyone in the relationship is self-centered and void of zeal or passion for their marriage, it will eventually end (even if the couple stays together). Where there is no wood the fire goes out and where there is no water there will be no life.

First, take a good look at your relationship and identify what category below your marriage fits in.

1. Fascinating
   a. Capable of arousing or holding interest - interesting, absorbing, arresting, thought-provoking, desirable, engrossing, eye-catching, intriguing, provocative
   b. Enthralling, mesmerizing, alluring, captivating, charming, arouses the interest and attention of.

2. Rewarding
    a. Affording fulfillment, worthwhile, pleasing, good, gratifying, agreeable,
    b. Advantageous, profitable, enjoyable, pleasurable
3. Satisfying
    a. To undergo an examination or trial with favorable results. Passing, achieving, accomplishing, cutting it, making it,
    b. To be satisfactory to. Answering, appeasing, cutting the mustard, making the grade, meeting, pleasing, being acceptable, suiting
4. Maintaining
    a. Working and caring for.
    b. Attending, feeding, looking after, ministering to, nursing, providing for, servicing, supporting, sustaining, waiting upon, keeping, nourishing, nurturing, taking care of,
    c. Continuing, preserving, retaining, upholding
5. Struggling
    a. An earnest try. Endeavoring, attempting, undertaking, venturing,
    b. Contending with difficulties and acting to overcome them. Coping, sparing, wrestling, striving,
    c. To strive in opposition to. Battling, colliding, combating, dueling, fighting, warring, wrestling, tugging
6. Disappointing
    a. Below the expected standard. Unsatisfactory, inadequate, unsatisfying, poor, wanting,
    b. To prevent from being successful. Foiled, thwarted, frustrated, hindered, prevented, baffled, circumvented,

c. To fail to satisfy the expectations or wishes of. Discontented, disenchanted, disgruntled, disheartened, disillusioned, dissatisfied, let down
7. Distressing
   a. Difficult or impossible to tolerate or bear.
   b. Intolerable, upsetting, hurting, painful, unbearable, worrying, or sad,
   c. Verbal abuse, physical abuse, violent, cruelty, neglecting, misusing, mistreatment or harsh.

Next, be true to yourself and your spouse and write down the reasons you think you are in that category.

Follow that by having a conversation with your spouse to discuss the categories you, as a couple, do well in. Dig deeper into your relationship with conversations on the areas that need improvement. Then allow time for both of you to explain why you feel you all are where you are. Be sure to take turns and listen while the other is talking.

Last, provide solutions to the areas you all feel you can correct or adjust to improve your relationship to be able to come alongside one another. Sometimes it may be best to have a "start over" with the relationship you have with your spouse if you have fallen in the bottom three categories.

Go back and reset, begin anew, with a fresh new beginning. Start purposefully dating again as if you were just meeting for the first time while using the wisdom you have learned in this marriage handbook. Talk about the things you learned and set new goals. Learn how to have fun together all over again.

IDENTIFY WHERE YOU ARE

It may be uncomfortable or awkward at first, but with God's love and forgiveness on your side you can make your marriage work. Better than it was before, stronger, more durable.

Many couples have come to know that it does not take much to grow apart with everything in life moving so fast. If you do not keep it together intentionally your relationship will surely drift away. So, make doable solutions to keep mending your marriage to keep it intact. Never stop loving your spouse.

Be sure to monitor your progress by tracking your results and check your list on an agreed upon interval to see what type of progress you all are making or maintaining. Set up an appointment with a marriage counselor to help if necessary.

And be sure to treat yourselves when you both feel you have improved in a category or raised a category. Enjoy a movie, dinner, vacation, each other, or all of the above to celebrate the victory of unity.

With hard work and selflessness, any good marriage can be maintained, and any broken marriage can be fixed.

CHAPTER 21

UNTIL THE END

Life is a journey and marriage an experience, so know where you want to go and surround yourself with people who will help you reach your destination.

Enjoy the ride but be sure to perform marital preventive maintenance instead of unnecessary marital repair. Stay in remembrance that true love in a marriage must be tended to throughout the entirety of the marriage. You should want to be inseparable instead of feeling stuck. If you marry the right person for you, you will not have that to worry about.

Our pastor used to stress to all the married couples and couples to be: "Whatever you did to get your spouse is what you should be willing to do to keep your spouse. Do not change your actions unless it is for the better of the both of you."

The other meaning of the words "to cleave" in Genesis 2:24 is "to chase" or "to stick to like glue." Husbands need to keep chasing their wives and wives need to stay chasable.

Marriage is not all about one person and their self-image. Both parties must stay concerned about the relationship and stay connected without conditions.

Conditions have stipulations and anticipations associated with them. And when you add an "if" in your sacrifice statement or commitment clause, or "why" to I love you, you have set yourself up for a letdown because it then becomes conditional love. You are saying that your love is predicated on a condition (long hair, green eyes, plenty of money, a big house, an expensive car, handsomeness, or if you do me good).

It is okay to state a preference, but never make it a stipulation. In many cases you must make a choice between having babies and keeping the wife's super sexy shape intact; raising kids or having freedom and personal space; a two-parent income or a spotless house and dinner cooked every night.

God's love for His spouse is unconditional and therefore yours should be also. You do not always deserve God's love, but He loves you despite your shortcomings and inconsistencies.

Therefore, if God never said why He loves you and loves you unconditionally, then who are you to add stipulations and anticipations to your love for your spouse. Stipulations may lead to later frustrations, which can lead to arguments, which can lead to anger, which may lead to choice words, and if not put in perspective, separation and/or divorce.

Seven Common Misconceptions:

- Learning to love is automatic

- Every house is a home
- In-love keeps a marriage together
- Love is based on your feelings
- Having a baby will make you love each other
- Your marriage must be like your parents'
- Just because you are involved in grown folk business does not always mean you are mentally mature

Seven Tips To Keep Your Marriage in the Top 7:

- Keep open and honest communication a priority
- Never stop learning about you, your spouse and life
- Learn to speak and read your spouse's love language
- Embrace an attitude of daily forgiveness
- Learn to love despite how you feel
- Know the value of romantic love and work on it
- Do unto your spouse as you would like for them to do unto you

Seven Phrases of Wisdom for those Planning on Getting Married

- Success is directly proportional to one's preparation
- Marriage can make or break a person's soul (mind, conscious, will, intellect, emotions, and passions)
- Marriage is a choice and not involuntary
- Responsibility is the qualifier and not age
- Money does not buy happiness
- Marriage is not necessary for you to fulfill your God given purpose

MARRIAGE PLANS FOR TWO

- Marriage is the first institution God created and is ordained by God and not man. So, take your vows seriously.

Seven reasons why you (the husband) should keep chasing your wife:

- You do not want her to get away
- She wants you to
- You want to
- You do not want anyone else to catch her
- The before and after exercise is favorable
- The benefits are incredible
- You love her

Seven reasons why you (the wife) should stay chasable to your husband:

- You want him to keep chasing you
- You want him to stay
- You want to stay attractive to him (inside and out)
- You want his attention to be focused on you
- You take pride in who you are and how you look
- The subsidies are amazing
- You love him

7 "Cons..." to concentrate on:

- Be CONsiderate
- Know the CONsequences
- Extinguish CONflicts
- Avoid CONfusion

- Watch your CONduct
- Listen to your CONscience
- Stay in CONtrol

Happy marriages are intentional outcomes where two people purposely go beyond only saying "we are together" and willfully and deliberately become one to attain the desired goal of staying together.

You started with a proposed dream. Turned it into an ambitious idea; worked together until it became a meaningful plan; then got married and made your aspirations your purpose; allowed your aim to become your intent and consciously interact to keep building a sustainable, bonded relationship that will endure to the end of your time on Earth.

To the husbands: Ecclesiastes 9:9-10 (KJV):

9. Live joyfully with the wife whom thou lovest all the days of the life of thy vanity, which he hath given thee under the sun, all the days of thy vanity: for that is thy portion in this life, and in thy labour which thou takest under the sun.

10. Whatsoever thy hand findeth to do, do it with thy might; for there is no work, nor device, nor knowledge, nor wisdom, in the grave, whither thou goest.

To the wives: Proverbs 31: 10-12, 28 (KJV):

10. Who can find a virtuous woman? for her price is far above rubies.

11. The heart of her husband doth safely trust in her, so that he shall have no need of spoil.

12. She will do him good and not evil all the days of her life.

28. Her children arise up, and call her blessed; her husband also, and he praiseth her.

TOGETHER FOREVER is what we pray for in your **"MARRIAGE PLANS FOR TWO."**

EXTRAS TO ENJOY

Chapters 22 - 24

CHAPTER 22

THE MASCULINE MARKER
Together

There are many challenges in life with great rewards if you are victorious. The challenge to find your wife ranks in the top three. There are approximately 170 million females in the United States and more than 3.7 billion females in the world. Your objective is to obtain the one that was purposed for you. You will have to be intentional and locate and acquire your wife instead of mistakenly choosing a female designed to be someone else's wife. The end goal is for the two of you to be TOGETHER. Be very discreet, stick with the plan and remember:

When you realize it is
HER-TO-GET
You make it your agenda to
GET-TO-HER
And you do what you have to do
TO-GET-HER
So, you all can forever be

TOGETHER

And before you go you should check your A.I.M. (Agenda, Intentions and Motives) for getting a wife.

- Are you looking for a lifelong companion or a mama with benefits (sex only)?
- Are you in need of fulfillment or a place to stay?
- Are you hoping to make someone happy or checking off a task on your bucket list?
- Are you seeking a wife or a baby maker?
- Are you in the process of looking for someone to unconditionally love or for someone to go in half with the bills and household responsibilities?
- Your A.I.M. should be "looking for your soul mate" to love her and be together for ever. Congratulations to the men who have accomplished this first phase.

Genesis 2:18 (KJV):
18. And the Lord God said, It is not good that the man should be alone; I will make him an help meet for him.

Man did not decide he needed a wife. God did! God knew the creation He created. He created the man for fellowship. The man was designed to express love. First vertically and then horizontally. It was for that reason that God gave man a gift called woman and made her his wife. God knew His design was whole but incomplete (spiritually and naturally). His goal was to create an appropriate and satisfactory help meet for the man.

The wife was designed to be a suitable helper that compliments, balances, satisfies and completes the man to whom she is joined. She was not created to be his servant. She was to be a companion that he would treat equally, cover willingly, and love unconditionally.

So, when God performed the first surgery and took the rib from the man to make the woman, He was creating an extension of the man with a specific purpose in mind. Husbands, your wife is your rib, and she has a purpose for being in your life. The three main purposes of ribs in the body are: 1) Protection, 2) Support, and 3) Respiration.

- Protection: ribs protect the heart, lungs, spleen, and liver. A Christian wife covers her husband in prayer as his protector. She loves him and stands up for him. A wife should know her husband better than anyone else if she is to defend him. She has or will learn his strengths and weaknesses so others cannot take advantage of him. The husband must allow his wife to earn his trust so she could help protect him and be his shield from exposure, injury, damage, and destruction. She will be a force where the devil cannot entrap her husband and where people who intend to do him harm cannot get to him.
- Support: ribs are the framework for the shoulder, chest, back and upper abdominal muscles to attach to. A wife could never be a husband, but she is the framework that God designed to hold him up and in place. She is strong enough for him to lean on and compassionate enough to comfort her husband when life and circumstances are either good or

bad. It takes two for a dynamic duo so husbands should not let their pride get in the way of working together with his wife in all things.
- Respiration: ribs are made flexible to expand and contract while assisting in breathing. This definition says it all when it comes to a wife as a marriage partner. A good wife gives her husband a reason to breathe and room to breathe. Respiration, by definition, is a physical and chemical process where energy is obtained when you join two things and get a release. What is so hard about that reaction? Our point exactly. That is how a husband spells relief (r-e-l-e-a-s-e). And that is what he calls great respiration. And just one of the many ways a wife can give aid and help her husband. The wife provides the fire, and the husband will supply the sacrifice.

Proverbs 5:19 (KJV):
19. Let her be as the loving hind and pleasant roe; let her breasts satisfy thee at all times; and be thou ravished always with her love.
Ecclesiastes 9:9 (KJV):
9. Live joyfully with the wife whom thou lovest all the days of the life of thy vanity,

My cook of love - how to cook your bib

Food for thought:

For you to maximize your love life for a lifetime and be a "rib" specialist you must be like a master chef cooking in an elegant and expensive fine dining restaurant when it comes to pleasing your wife.

How to attain rib specialist status:

- Season her well with oils (perfumes and/or lotion)
- Rub her down on the outside first and then the inside
- Inject her, marinate her, and then slow cook her at the right temperature
- When her juices flow, baste her with your homemade sauce
- When her biological timer sounds off and the meat falls off the bone you have cooked your rib to the delight of your spouse
- Compliments to a happy chef

If you cook her right, she will love you even more.

Alternative cooking suggestions to please your wife and avoid kitchen nightmares:

- Only use the microwave when she wants it quick.
- Broil it when she wants it hot and, in a hurry,
- Grill it when she wants you to stand up and cook it.
- Smoke it when she has the time and has a taste for flavor
- Bake it when she wants it tender and at a set degree

Leave your culinary marker on your wife as a hallmark note to identify your artistry, affection, appreciation, and appetency.

What 5 things was most important to you when searching for your wife?

1.

2.

3.

4.

5.

CHAPTER 23

THE FEMININE FINGERPRINT
Manifesto

A manifesto is defined as a public statement. When a woman says I am getting married to or am married to someone, she is making an announcement that says a lot about herself. She is saying that out of the 160 million males in America and over 3 billion males in the world; I choose or have chosen this one.

Your preliminary goal is to make sure you find and acquire the husband God created for you instead of settling for a husband that God created for someone else.

Wife, your ultimate goal is to proclaim that the MAN-I-FES-TO is my manifesto that you will love and cherish for your lifetime. Your husband is the man that you will confess and share all your innermost thoughts and desires with because he is the man you trust. And congratulations to the women who have found just that in their man.

You have proclaimed to the world who you wanted to be faithful to when you said "I do" on your wedding day. You did not say why you did what you did, but you did make a manifesto to be together forever.

Hopefully, you checked your A.I.M. before you said I do. AIM, (Agendas, Intentions and Motives), are vital in everyday life and extremely important when you are getting married.

- Are you looking for happiness or someone to fill your void until... (sex only)?
- Are you in need of a forever friend or free housing?
- Are you confirming what is in your heart or doing what your friends did?
- Do you want a honeymoon, or your moon honeyed?
- Are you seeking a husband or a baby daddy?
- Are you in the process of looking for someone to unconditionally love or for someone to get you the things you want?

Your A.I.M. should be "looking for your soul mate" and be ready to love him with your all until death parts the two of you.

Genesis 2:18 lets us know that the woman did not decide she needed the man as her companion. God said so. A woman was created and designed to be the expression of love. She is to express her love vertically and then horizontally. Women are the greatest gift that God gave to men.

And if God had His way, they would stay wrapped until the vows are complete. As a woman, you come packaged with treats and dainties that some men live for, and others are willing to go to the extreme for.

Therefore, you must understand your power and your gift. You were designed to be a companion that willingly chooses to bring out the best in the man you choose to marry. You are not his maid or attendant. You are his help meet that is built to complete him. You are of great value and essential to the plan of God. So, take your place, fulfill your role, and position yourself for greatness as you make a statement. You were created to be a solution, not a problem. Man was alone and incomplete until a woman was made to be his rib.

As the rib, your husband is your covering and protection. His presence should bring a sense of protection for you and your children as you protect, support, and allow your husband the freedom to breath. As a Christian wife you shelter your husband in prayer as his integrity defends your honor. Stand in the gap and fight to ensure that he is protected as he provides a safe place for you and his family. You have what he needs to be successful so embrace your position. You provide for your family and keep them safe from dangers seen and unseen as your husband stands in the gap and deals with guarding the house so it can remain a home.

Your support is vital. Not only in building your husband up, but also in holding him up as well. Great wives give their husbands space to breathe without smothering him or being too pushy. You volunteered for the function of being his wife, so keep the vows that you made.

My cook of love - how to work the oven:

MARRIAGE PLANS FOR TWO

Making a MANIFESTO is what you did when you joined yourself as your husband's help meet. But your public statement must be manifested in private as you learn how to operate your God given gift. You were designed with a built-in masterwork and must learn how to operate it to mesmerize your husband and captivate his attention and please his appetite for a lifetime of love. Your oven masterpiece is designed to transform and complete what is undone and satisfy your husband's appetite.

How to be a top-of-the-line work of art:

- Look good on the outside and have true value on the inside
- Have easy access knobs to turn the temperature up
- Come with an element at the bottom for cooking or baking and an element at the top for broiling
- Use the adjustable racks to get your husband to the desired temperature for his enjoyment
- Be confident in knowing that your oven was built far more superior than the gift your husband wishes to present

Woman note: the man was built strong on the outside, but the woman was created stronger on the inside. The exterior muscles and strength of most men can overpower and outperform most women. But man's advantage of physical powerfulness ends when compared to the inner design and muscles of the woman. The internals of a woman are far more adaptable than the man. And contrary to most men beliefs, she was designed to be far more sexually superior to her counterpart. The woman was deliberately constructed to be incredibly amazing.

- They can bear life and allow it to grow and live on the inside

- They can birth a lengthy, multi-pound child and return to their original condition
- They can produce milk to feed a child
- They can naturally lose blood and still be physically healthy
- They were designed to receive what their husbands have to offer and give it back to them in a way that makes him happier than when he gave it

A man's exterior gift is like a Rolex watch and a woman's internal gifts are like Timex watches. When a Rolex watch is hit too hard it sometimes loses its function for a while, but a Timex watch keeps on ticking.

Leave your fingerprint impressions on your husband as a featured stamp of your affection, attribution, quality, and character.

What 5 things was most important to you when searching for your husband?

1.

2.

3.

4.

5.

CHAPTER 24

IMMINENT VISUALIZATIONS

THE ROOM

L. Tillery

Imagine a room....

A ROOM IN YOUR MIND CALLED - MARRIAGE

A beautiful room. A room designed to intrigue, awe, and inspire. A fantasy room. A room full of possibilities where your dreams can come true if you apply yourself. An entertainment room. A room full of happiness, fun and pleasure. A possibility room. A room where you have the power and potential to choose success or failure. A practice room. A room where you train by repetition to become competent and committed. A war room. A room where you can plan and strategize how to overcome your enemies and obstacles. A together room. A room for two people, and two people only that have decided to become one. A commitment room. A room where you make vows to enter and pay money to leave. An opportunity room. A room where you can make the best of life with the person you chose to be with in this room. A consent room. A room where you volunteer to go in and volunteer to stay.

Envision a room with only two doors. One door on one side of the room and one door on the opposite side of the room. A room with doors in the corners diagonally across from one another. A room where you can only enter in one door but can exit out of two.

Can you conceive being in a room with a permanent D on one door and a temporary D on the other? A room where you are educated about the doors before you come in and really conceptualize them after you gain admission. A room where you enter through the door that is marked wedding. A room that is designed for you to exit, over time, through the door marked "Death" on the opposite side of the room. A room where it is not advised to exit out of the door marked "Divorce" (which is the back side of the door you used to enter the room). A room of hope and love that causes the two of you to tell the doorkeeper to install a deadbolt to secure the door of divorce from the outside where it cannot be opened from the inside.

Visualize yourself in a room now with one option closed shut and one option wide open, and both options being undesirable by the two in the room. It is a perfect room for two. A bonding room. A green room with no limits. A love room where the flames of romance can ignite and warm the room with affection.

A fluctuating room at times. A changing room with the possibility of unexpected temperature shifts. An uneasy room where the colder the two become to each other, the hotter the

IMMINENT VISUALIZATIONS

room will be. Picture yourself standing there in the now uncomfortable room. And the sparks from the two start a fire in the room. A room of decision as the wildfire rages. One room where the two will have three choices, two doors and one good solution.

Choice one - choose to do nothing, and by doing so automatically choose the door of death. Together in a room but not together. Lethargically choosing to sit there in a deteriorating room as time goes by until they eventually go into eternity by age or by choice. Individually or at the same time.

Choice two - choose to try and open the door of divorce that you chose to bolt shut because you pledged not to go that route. But will it be worth the pain and agony experienced by everyone when you damage the room by opening the divorce door? And if you do not hurry up and make a choice, you will choose choice one because if the smoke of discord does not smother you, the flames or rage will burn you. Therefore, choice two is not an advisable option, leaving you with the best solution - choice three.

Choice three - choose to WORK TOGETHER, put the fire out, restore the room, repair the damages, live peacefully, enjoy each other, and be ready to fight another fire on another day.

A settled room. An emotion-filled room. A secure room. A transformational room. An experience room. A laboring room. A process room. A room built for two to become one.

……Can you see the image of "The Room?"

THE FORBIDDEN FRUIT
L. Tillery

I purchased a field and on it came a tree.
My very own wife for no one but me.
She shared all her fruits each day and night.
I sold out and loved her with all of my might.

Oh, the happiness we shared as we became one.
The promises we made until our lives were done.
How the branches would reach out and meet our needs.
How we would produce and raise each of our seeds.

Everything was well and life was just great.
The roots grew deeper as I enjoyed my soul mate.
Through the seasons of summer, fall, winter and spring.
We looked forward to new memories that time would bring.

But one day an unexpected opportunity came.
The devil disguised himself as a delightful dame.
Honeycomb lips with a mouth smoother than oil.
My happy home is what she purposed to spoil.

An adulteress woman with a flattering tongue.

MARRIAGE PLANS FOR TWO

Words of deceit in the songs that she sung.
Passion and lust I saw in her eyes.
Urgency and desire I heard in her cries.

Luscious to the touch and taste were her beauty.
Seduction and destruction had become her duty.
The aroma of fragrances on her I did smell.
She was hot like the fire of a burning hell.

The forbidden fruit was alive and real.
My relationship with God she wanted to steal.
The love for my wife she wanted me to put aside.
And in her bosom of immorality, she wanted me to abide.

At this junction in life, I had to count the costs.
What would I gain if my soul was lost?
I could be forgiven seventy times seven.
But my goal in life was to make it to heaven.

Therefore, the option wasn't even a choice.
I prayed to God in a very loud fervent voice.
Help me be victorious over the temptation to sin.
The devil is a liar and my soul he'll never win.

Why should I be filled by any forbidden fruit?
And must keep it silent until I'm given the boot.
When at home I have a basket created just for me.
With the fruit and its juices arranged so delicately.

THE FORBIDDEN FRUIT

> I'll rejoice with the wife of my youth always.
> Her breast will satisfy me all of my days.
> I'll forever be ravished with her sweet love.
> And I'll continually be faithful to God up above.
>
> Her fruit and fountain will fill my heart.
> And I refuse to let anything tear us apart.
> Her peaches, plums, cherries, and grapes.
> Will bless me, fulfill me, and keep me in her gates.
>
> Marriage is honorable and the bed undefiled.
> Adultery is a sin where lusts have gone wild.
> Forbidden fruit and stolen waters seem so sweet.
> Until I stand before Jesus at the judgement seat.
>
> So, the field I purchased with the charming tree on it.
> Is the fruit I picked and her pleasures I'll always get.
> Let my wife be as the loving hind and pleasant roe.
> And only in her garden bed shall I ever go.

Fidelity is simply putting your priorities in perspective. It protects the investment both stakeholders made in the partnership. **Choose your path forward and be careful to stay the course.**

"Loving Your Lineage"

We close with these words of wisdom. Marriages do not just start intimate relationships; they usually start families in the series of events that follow. Therefore, the couple should endeavor to be good examples to their children. They must demonstrate wholesome relational and parenting skills.

God intended for the family to be a close-knit unit integrated to assist one another for the good of each other and the betterment of everyone's quality of life. Family is a choice that should be taken seriously. No matter how you became a family, intentional or by accident, you should value your Family.

It's your choice. You can stay single for the rest of your life if you choose. And single means you and only you. But the moment you add spouse and/or children to your resume you are no longer considered single.

Family Dynamics:

- **Couple**: Romantically paired (no children)
- **Traditional Family:** 2 parents rearing children they conceived together
- **Single Parent Family:** 1 parent rearing children
- **Blended Family:** 2 parents rearing children from previous relationships

We strongly recommend that everyone totally understand two very important words before they decide to leave their singleness. Love and commitment. And if that has changed before now; then we strongly recommend you pay particular attention to incorporate these two important words into your family life. Love always includes a sacrifice and an offering. Commitment always includes an obligation and a contract.

Church, community leaders, family and friends can assist in providing supplemental guidance and support to your children. "It takes a village to raise a child." But it is ultimately the parent(s) sole responsibility to ensure that their child(ren) is nurtured and raised correctly.

Proverbs 22:6 (KJV):
"Train up a child in the way he should go: and when he is old, he will not depart from it."
TRAINING = TEACHING + TALKING + TIME

We believe a family's success mainly hinges on three specific mechanisms with each one providing three primary components. (We call it the LTs 3X3 rules for successful families):

1. Community
2. Children
3. Parents

COMMUNITIES

The responsibilities of the Community:

-Communities should provide good **Environments, Education, and Economics**. It has been said, "everyone is a product of their environment." Therefore, communities should strive to provide hope for a better tomorrow for each member of the family. The city must provide resources to teach their communities to be well rounded in their academic, economic, social, and personal lives as they strive for overall success.

"The solution is to make a proclamation and a resolution for dedication to higher education so we can make preparation for the next generation."

Proverbs 1:8 (KJV):
"My son, hear the instruction of thy father, and forsake not the law of thy mother:"

CHILDREN

The responsibilities of the child(ren):

Children should exercise good **Discipline, Determination and Discretion**. Contrary to popular belief; everyone has a role to play in creating a successful family, even the children. They must be ambitious, self-controlled, decisive, obedient, teachable, disciplined, and strong enough to resist peer pressure.

PARENTS

We will go into further detail with parenting because this will be directly related to you and your spouse's future obligations.

The responsibilities of the parents:

Parents should deliver good Standards, Structure and Support.

STANDARDS help children meet expectations. They are established policies, procedures, or rules that one follows to accomplish preset objectives or goals. They are best taught by setting general and specific expectations and then holding the children accountable to act in accordance with them.

Examples of Standards:
Principles, Values, Morals, Ethics, Character, Expectations, Acceptable Behaviors.

STRUCTURE helps children achieve balance in life. It is a developmental process that teaches discipline, consistency, and organization. It is best learned by example, in a stable environment, which demonstrates fundamental principles to children of all ages.

Examples of Structure:
Vision, Goals, Order, Direction
How to Plan, Prepare, Strategize,
How to be Effectual, Systematic and Methodical by the EXAMPLE the parent sets.

SUPPORT assists children in achieving explicit objectives. It is the love, caring or concern demonstrated by another that motivates one to excel because of a sense of belonging or relevance. Support is best established when actively participating in events that children are engaged in.

Examples of Support:
Participation in their school or sports activities, Encouragement, Instruction, Advice, Wise Counsel, Guidance, Assistance (Physical and Financial), Motivation, Inspiration, Time.

Believe it or not, people (especially children) will do things they would not ordinarily do for people who they have a desire to please. We believe it is of the upmost importance to build great relationships with your children to help them develop properly.

Your children should be given the basic necessities of life and living (love, security, food, water, shelter, and a sense of belonging). Parents must take their roles seriously and know when to be firm and when to be flexible. It is advisable for parents to play the role of good "project managers" when children are dependent and still living at home. The parents' roles should change to that of "consultants" when their children move away from home in search of self-sufficiency.

A true family is a TEAM. Everyone must fulfill their respective part for the good of the whole instead of being selfish individuals. If the team falls short in one area, the family unit may suffer disharmony.

As a parent, you can help, handicap, or hurt your children by projecting your outlook and objectives. A parent can help their child by teaching them to be independent. A parent can handicap their child by teaching them to be dependent. Or a parent can hurt their child by teaching them to be withdrawn.

Proverbs 17:6 (KJV):
"Children's children are the crown of old men; and the glory of children are their fathers."

Remember, A mother's love is worth more than money can buy, and it is well documented that children fare better with their dads in their lives.

Parents, love your children.

Husbands, love your wives.

Wives, Cherish your husbands.

Never stop loving one another.

But first and foremost,

Keep making

"MARRIAGE PLANS FOR TWO"

BIOGRAPHIES

Lenard Tillery, Jr and Lisa's blissful marital union began on June 10, 1989. To this union, six amazing children were born (Lauren, LaKaley, Lenard III, Lindsey, Lexie and LeNae). They faithfully served their late pastor for 26 years and are currently the founders of The Example Church in Baker, Louisiana where Pastor and Lady Tillery minister.

Lenard and Lisa were both born and educated in New Orleans, Louisiana. As divine destiny would have it, their journeys crossed when they met at a bible study while attending college in Baton Rouge, Louisiana. God's anointing and assignment directed them to passionately work in multiple ministries as outreach directors, cell group leaders, marriage retreat organizers, conference speakers,' pastoral assistants, and anointed soul winners.

Lady Lisa Tillery enjoys being a wife, mother, and motivational speaker. She has a bachelor's degree in Business with an emphasis in accounting, and also earned a Master of Business Administration degree.

Pastor Lenard Tillery enjoys time with his family and writing. He is the author of two books, "What is Man?' and "Not Too Easy." He received his bachelor's degree in Construction Management and when he answered the call to Pastor, he went back to college to earn his master's degree in Pastoral Counseling (Marriage and Family cognate).

We are dedicated to helping you achieve greatness in your marriage. Our team has provided the information in this instruction manual to make **YOUR TEAM** better.

Smell your flowers and watch your relationship bloom. Let your providence become your paradise and your passion become your purpose. It is your provision for your prepared planning. It's **YOUR TEAM** now.

Stop just imagining your dream and allow your goals to become reality. Begin the project to love your proposed marriage life as you make **MARRIED PLANS FOR TWO**.

Visit us at www.lenardtillery.com

Pastor Lenard and Lady Lisa Tillery

Made in the USA
Middletown, DE
03 February 2023

23203725R00106